Debt-Proof
Your Marriage

WORKBOOK

Debt-Proof Your Marriage

WORKBOOK

Mary Hunt

Fleming H. Revell
A Division of Baker Book House Co
Grand Rapids, Michigan 49516

© 2003 by Mary Hunt

Published by Fleming H. Revell
a division of Baker Book House Company
P.O. Box 6287, Grand Rapids, MI 49516-6287
www.bakerbooks.com

Printed in the United States of America

ISBN 0-8007-5849-8 (pbk.)

Contents

Part 3 Unique Solutions for Common Dilemmas

How to Use This Workbook

This *Debt-Proof Your Marriage Workbook* can be used in a variety of ways.

- You will get the most out of this workbook if you and your spouse read the book *Debt-Proof Your Marriage* first. It's an easy read, and hopefully you will find it semi-entertaining. Reading through the book will give both of you the opportunity to see the big picture without getting bogged down and sidetracked with detours and homework. You'll have the equivalent of a literary "aerial" shot of the journey on which you are about to embark. Once you have a good grasp of what it means to debt-proof your marriage—and the assurance that it will be a joyful journey, not one to be dreaded—you'll be ready to jump into this workbook together, using the text as your guide and reference. Or . . .

- Together you can jump right in with *Debt-Proof Your Marriage* in one hand and this workbook in the other, working one chapter at time, using the text to flesh out key concepts and relying on real-life examples to encourage more thorough discussion of important points. Or . . .

- You can use either of the methods above to do this on your own in the event your spouse is not interested at this time. That's okay. His or her reluctance should not prevent you from going ahead. The only person necessary to begin to move your relationship toward a place of intimacy and financial harmony is you. You can effect the beginning of significant change in your marriage and if necessary you can do that single-handedly. Or . . .

- You and your spouse can be part of a small group that meets regularly to discuss the financial challenges you face in your marriages in addition to working through the text and workbook on your own.

You're about to learn that I enjoy asking questions. In fact, I have a good friend who has chided me for many years, insisting that I ask too many questions (you know who you are, Duane). If you agree, slow down. Take only one question or section at a time, and then come back later for more. Give yourselves time to digest and ponder before going on. Or skip some questions and come back later. Just keep this in mind: *The questions you'd rather not answer are likely the ones you need to answer the most.* Just take your time. And use a pencil. You may want to go back and make changes to your responses as you allow the process to develop your thinking.

Each chapter includes "Pillow Talk." This is a topic for the two of you to discuss during your most quiet and alone time. Here are the Pillow Talk guidelines: No criticism, correcting, probing, or contradiction. It is important that both of you feel safe, accepted, and free to respond because you know nothing you say will be used against you.

Most of the questions provide enough space for a single answer from each of you. If you prefer to answer separately, no problem. You'll just have to use your own paper to supplement the space provided. When it seems more appropriate to me for you to answer individually, the question is followed by "He says" and "She says."

I hope you will make a commitment to one another that this book will be sacred property between just the two of you. Knowing that it is for your four eyes only will give you the assurance and confidence that you need so you can share your heart without fear of outside intrusion.

Above all, I hope you will enjoy the process. I'm enjoying the thought of the two of you caring enough about the other and your marriage to do what may at times seem like hard work.

My hope is that this work will strengthen your relationship and deepen your love for each other as you develop financial harmony in your marriage.

Introduction

The subtitle of this workbook is *How to Achieve Financial Harmony*. I come from a musical background, so while the dictionary might assign a broad spectrum of definitions and applications to the word *harmony*, my mind goes to the process of blending compatible musical tones to make luscious, rich sounds. How do you define harmony?

Now think of harmony in relation to your personal financial situation. How do you think that would look? How will you recognize financial harmony in your marriage?

You may have read books, purchased software, attended seminars, or enrolled in a program at your church or in your community. Your attempts may have worked in the beginning, but then, like a failed diet, you go back to the old ways and experience the equivalent of gaining back all of the weight you lost, plus some. (p. 9)*

*Text in extracts or quotations marks is from the book *Debt-Proof Your Marriage*. Page references to *Debt-Proof Your Marriage* are in parentheses.

Why are you reading *Debt-Proof Your Marriage,* and what do you hope to accomplish?

What attempts, if any, have you made in the past to figure out your finances and manage money in your marriage?

I'm going to take a big leap here and assume those attempts were not successful because you are reading this book. Why do you think those attempts failed to deliver the results you desired? Was it the information, or was it the relationship?

What is the *precondition* (p. 10) for developing the most effective financial harmony in your marriage?

Every couple experiences conflict in their marriage from time to time. That's normal and a healthy aspect of marriage. Some conflicts are minor or "surface" matters (p. 10), while others are of a much deeper nature. Conflicts are not the problem. The problem is when these conflicts do not find resolution. Generally speaking, how do you resolve conflicts in your marriage? Do you have some that have never been resolved? Explain.

"Money in a marriage is not simply about money" (p. 9). Money conflicts in marriage are usually the symptom of conflicts of a deeper nature, having to do with broken trust and unmet needs. If money conflicts are rooted in something deeper, do you agree or disagree that more money will only mask, not resolve, these problems? Explain.

Part I

Get Your Relationship Ready for Financial Harmony

I

This Is My Story, and I'm Sticking to It

Everyone has a story. Everything you've done, every place you've been, and everything you've experienced, good or bad, even if you cannot recall the details, has made you the person you are today.

Every time I reflect on my story (p. 15), I am astonished all over again that even the unlovely parts of our lives can be transformed into something useful. The fact that I now spend my life helping others get control of their finances and debt-proof their lives is an irony not unlike a drug dealer becoming a pharmacist or a stuttering child a speech therapist.

"In the years we dated, I never tipped my hand about my little spending problem. He might think poorly of me. Besides, it was absolutely unnecessary. Once we were married, that would be my private history, the old me" (p. 17). Or so I thought. But I couldn't hide the truth for long.

TO DO

Using two different colors of ink (one for her responses, another for his), place a check mark beside every statement that describes your perception(s) prior to marriage:

1. I'm really bad with money.
2. Once we're married I'll never have to worry about money again.
3. I plan to keep some things to myself . . . forever. She/he will never have to know about my financial past. I'll figure out how to fix it later.
4. I'm a little worried about what's going to happen to my excellent credit rating.
5. I'm not at all worried about money. Everything will work out.
6. This is going to be like getting a raise because we'll have two incomes instead of only one.
7. We'll keep our money separate because I just don't trust him/ her with my money.
8. I know she/he will change her/his ways once we're married.
9. I was so young and naive I didn't have any money perceptions, positive or negative. I just didn't think about it.
10. If we can qualify for the credit, that means we can afford to use it.

What, if any, money issues did you discover after you were married that made you wonder, "How did I miss that?" Explain.

"Getting our first bankcard was a defining moment that would reshape my life, and not for the better" (p. 18). What money-related event(s) became a life-defining moment for you, either before or after you were married?

I collected credit cards almost for sport. I wasn't really expecting to use them. I just wanted to prove that I could get them. How many credit cards do you estimate you've had in your lifetime between the two of you?

Has there been a time in your life when you, like I, came to the end of yourself? If so, what were the circumstances?

Pillow Talk

Tell your spouse about one money expectation or assumption that you brought to your marriage from our childhood. What was the source of that message (if you know)?

A Stiff Dose of Reality

Think back to the planning, preparations, work, money, time, and energy you put into your wedding and all the events that led to it.

How long did that take?

What was the total cost for everything wedding related?

If your wedding was paid for with credit, has it been repaid now?

Place a check mark next to the things you did to prepare for your marriage:

1. Took premarital counseling
2. Read self-help books
3. Attended relationship classes
4. Went to an engagement encounter workshop
5. Took personality tests and profiles
6. Traded our credit reports
7. Developed a budget
8. Talked about how we would manage our money
9. Settled our differences regarding debt and the use of credit
10. Other (list below)

Approximately how much money did you spend on these kinds of marriage-related preparations?

If the preparation, planning, and spending on the wedding equals 100 percent, make an estimate for how the preparation, planning, and spending on the *marriage* compares: _____ percent

The point is that most of us put all kinds of resources, both financial and emotional, into the wedding ceremony and reception, and assume the marriage will somehow take care of itself.

Current statistical research reveals that the number one killer of marriages and cause of divorce is _____ conflicts. The subject of the conflict that most often goes unresolved is _____. Is this a new fact for you, or have you suspected all along that money issues are a common problem in most marriages? Explain.

Using the information on pages 30–31 of the text, respond true or false to the following:

_____ 1. The only effective solution for serious unresolved money conflicts is divorce.
_____ 2. Children of divorce are at no greater risk statistically speaking than children from two-parent families.
_____ 3. The damaging effects of divorce on spouses and children are so immense, they cannot be calculated.
_____ 4. Of all parties to a divorce, surprisingly, it is the father who ultimately suffers the greatest drop in income and standard of living.
_____ 5. There are no winners in a divorce.

Contrary to what many people believe or dream, more money will not make us truly happy, with one exception. What is that one exception and condition under which more money will make a significantly positive difference?

On page 32, it says the likelihood of an unhappy marriage improving dramatically all on its own if the parties will just refuse to split up is quite high. Given your life experience, how do you respond to that statement; do you agree or disagree? Explain.

Research gives us a lot of information on what truly makes us happy in our marriages. Referring to the information on page 31, summarize what you now believe is the key to happiness in marriage.

Does the fact that a healthy marriage promotes financial success give you tremendous hope and desire to make your good marriage even better? Explain.

God created you with a need for close relationships, first with him and then with another person. How are you doing with these two important relationships? What can you do starting right now to nourish these relationships?
She says:

He says:

Pillow Talk

Time has made you much wiser. On your wedding day you repeated the vows and meant them with all your hearts. But time has given you greater understanding. In the quietness of your alone time together, renew those vows. Use your own words, or these classic vows from The Book of Common Prayer, *1552: "I take thee to have and to hold, from this day forward, for better for worse, for richer for poorer, in sickness and in health, to love and to cherish, till death do us part, according to God's holy ordinance and thereto I give thee my troth."*

Answers: (1) F, (2) F, (3) T, (4) F, (5) T

3

Marriage Is like a Dirt Road

Engineer Pass—two words that still send a chill down my spine. I've done a little research and have learned that more people on average perish in automobile incidents in a single day on the freeways of Los Angeles than on Engineer Pass in a decade.

Have you ever taken a terrifying trip? Can you see any parallels between that experience and your marriage? You'll need to lean heavily on your sense of humor perhaps, but list those parallels here.

Think back to your prewedding days, specifically your money assumptions and expectations. Were they anywhere close to reality, or were you in a state of fantasy?

In your own words, describe the 5 Stages of Marriage (pp. 37–42). Place a star next to the stage you believe best describes your marriage at this time.

Stage 1:

Stage 2:

Stage 3:

Stage 4:

Stage 5:

Paula and Ken: We naively assumed we'd get so many gifts of money we'd have enough to pay for our honeymoon, wedding, perhaps even our student loans, past due bills, rent, down payment on a house (we invited a lot of people!). But when we added it up it wasn't even enough to pay for the honeymoon suite at a posh hotel for our wedding night. Worse, we overdid it on the credit cards thinking we'd get enough to pay them off, too. Now many years later we are stuck with bigger bills than ever.

Jen and Jeff: We figured somehow we'd have enough money. All the married people we knew and watched in our growing up years seemed to do okay, like a Right of Marriage or something. Boy, did we have a rude awakening. They made it look so easy. Too bad we didn't think to research this a little further when we were still in a position to do something about it. Ten years later we're so deeply in debt it's difficult to see how we'll ever get out. Debt has put a horrible strain on our relationship. At least once a month one of us is tempted to just give up.

Do you know of any couples that are currently in Stage 5? What characteristics do they (or you, if you are that couple) have that lead you to believe this?

Can you see yourselves moving into Stage 5 or do you equate Stage 5 with age—only the elderly can achieve that level?

Pillow Talk

Using the Marriage Map (pp. 36-42), determine which stage your marriage is in. Is that where you want to be? If not, what can you do starting right now to move to your stage of choice?

4

The Currency of Life

Money exposes the differences in our personalities, the ways we were brought up, our money beliefs, and goals. The way we think about money and what we do with it reflects what we believe about it. But money issues are buried so deeply in our emotions, it is often difficult to know what we believe or where our money attitudes came from. And if you don't know a lot about yourself, it's likely you know even less about your spouse (p. 44).

In the little good news/bad news banter on pages 43–44 of the text, the bad news is that money has the greatest potential to ruin your relationship. What is the good news?

Remember back to your single days. Whether you were poor or prosperous, you took care of yourself and made all of your own decisions. Briefly describe what that was like.

You married. Things changed. Did money become an easier issue in your life because you had a partner to share the responsibility and the work, or did that complicate things? Explain with total honesty.

In the paragraph titled "The Currency of Life" on page 45 are quite a few definitions for money. Write five of those here, and describe how each of them relates to you personally:

1.

2.

3.

4.

5.

If you've ever studied temperaments and personality types, you may already have discovered which "type" you and your spouse are. Curiously one of you is likely more fascinated and interested in the subject than the other, which only proves the point that you really are different. However, for our purposes in debt-proofing your marriage, there are only two money personalities. Name them and then give a brief description of each.

Which are you? Your spouse? Expand your response by giving a few examples for both of you, sticking with just the facts. No criticism allowed.

"In a healthy marriage, the saver-spender combination creates balance. . . . Put a saver and a spender together in an unhealthy marriage, and watch the fireworks" (p. 47). Generally speaking, have the differences in your money personalities brought balance or fireworks to your marriage? Give evidence using several examples.

How do you think your marriage would change, if at all, if each of you would see the other's money personality as an asset rather than a liability?

Did the fact that money is considered a taboo subject in many homes and our society as a whole make it difficult for you to talk to your beloved about it prior to your marriage?

Has that taboo spilled over into your marriage to the extent that you find it difficult to talk about money now? If so, give some examples of that struggle and how it has manifested itself in your relationship.

On a scale of one to ten, where one is "pathetically ignorant" and ten is "highly confident and competent," how would you rate your own financial intelligence as evidenced by your past ability and willingness to manage your spending, save consistently, carry no unsecured debt, have a good handle on your credit report, and make sure your family is well-prepared for the future? Why?

How would you rate your spouse? Explain.

"Overindulged children often bring their attitudes of entitlement to adulthood. Conversely, children who grow up feeling financially deprived can also arrive at the front door of marriage determined that now they can have it all and are entitled to it, especially if that spouse believes the new spouse is the ticket to having it all" (p. 52). How do you think your family history affected your money temperament and behaviors? Explain.

Referring to "Money Myths" on page 53 of the text, fill in the partial lies or partial truths money tells us about these characteristics.

1. Achievement:

2. Freedom:

3. Respect:

4. Power:

5. Security:

6. Happiness:

Thinking back over the years of your marriage, have you lived as though any of these lies are true? Explain.

Marital infidelity. Most people equate infidelity with sexual affairs. However, there is another kind of infidelity in marriage: financial infidelity. What does financial infidelity mean to you?

List three scenarios that you believe fit your definition of financial infidelity. If you need an idea starter, here's one from my list: Having a secret credit card account.

Let's say you are saving money each week to buy your husband a Christmas gift. Of course, you do not want him to know. Would you consider this financial infidelity? Why or why not?

Let's say that your friends Hubert and Hilda (if you really do have friends by that name, it's a coincidence) are coming to terms with their finances after all these years. Hilda has spent years deceiving Hubert by running up a sizable amount of debt he knows nothing about. She wants to come clean but has no idea how to do this. How would you advise her, and what are the steps she should take?

What else would you tell Hilda?

Is it a sin to be angry? Explain your answer.

What typically happens to anger when it is swallowed or "stuffed"?

Has there been a time in your life when rather than dealing with the issues behind the anger, you stuffed it? What happened?

Name three ways to dissolve anger.

"Spouses expect to trust each other—financially, sexually, and emotionally. Stealing and dishonesty are things they need to watch for in the outside world, but certainly not within this intimate arrangement known as marriage" (p. 61). Are there financial secrets standing in the way of you having open communication with your spouse and an honest marriage? What are you going to do about it?

Pillow Talk

Unresolved anger can be deadly in a marriage. The first step is to acknowledge it. Gather all the courage you have and add it to the confidence and safety you feel for your spouse and tell him/her about that. You've been hauling that load far too long.

5

News Flash: You Are Different!

Your differences are likely what attracted you to one another and provided that "charm" factor during your courtship, engagement, and even through Stage 1 of your marriage.

Your differences are what make you such a great match—not identical spirits, but complementary, like two pieces of a puzzle. "You complete me!" is often the sentiment of starstruck lovers.

But in time what was so delightful in the early years becomes the reason many couples have conflicts. They are convinced that if they were exactly the same they would never disagree. I often receive letters in which the writer, after many years of marriage, tells me about his or her epiphany and the obvious reason for all of their problems: "We are so different!"

The truth is—and I hate to make this overly simplistic—men and women are different. Really different! And that's exactly the way it's supposed to be. Remember, acceptance and surrender are the hallmarks of Stages 4 and 5.

Describe the basic physiological differences between your brain and your spouse's:

Comparing men to waffles and women to spaghetti presents quite a word picture, doesn't it? Explain briefly why authors Bill and Pam Farrel make this analogy.

Do you see yourself and your spouse as waffles and spaghetti, or is that just a funny analogy that makes you hungry for maple syrup and garlic bread? Explain.

Using the information on pages 62–63 to get started, list several specific ways that you and your spouse are completely different.

Have your differences been the source of pain and conflict in your marriage in the past? Describe two or three that immediately come to mind.

If you've lamented your differences in the past, can you see the possibility of those differences becoming complementary and leading to harmony, specifically financial harmony in your marriage?

Using your best creative thinking, describe one or two of those possibilities.

Which do you believe plays a larger role in making money difficult for couples, temperament or gender? Why?

Every man and woman has three distinct parts, each with its own distinct need for fulfillment. What are they?

What are the signs that indicate a person is ignoring one or more of these distinct parts of his or her being?

You, like every person, have a deep need for loving relationships. What are the two areas of life that are strongly affected by the quality of your relationships, specifically your marital and family relationships?

Do you know or have you ever known of anyone who has attempted to substitute money for meaningful personal relationships? If so, how has that worked out for him/her?

Describe the effect when a person attempts to fill his or her needs for spiritual fulfillment with money and/or human relationships.

What is, or should be, the purpose of money, and what is its proper role in your life and marriage?

Prior to reading chapter 5, did you assume that your spouse's emotional needs were the same as yours, or is that something you'd just never thought about?

What need is high on every man's "Things I Need Most to Meet My Deep Emotional Needs" list and what is the best way that his wife and others in his life can meet that need?

Does respect hold that same high ranking on a woman's list? If not, what *does* rank very high on her list of deep emotional needs?

What do spouses do instinctively to meet each other's deep emotional needs?

What happens when a wife's needs go unmet because rather than giving her what she needs, her husband is giving to her what he wants from her?

What happens when a husband's needs go unmet because rather than giving him what he needs, his wife is giving to him what she wants from him?

Name the two ways any spouse can create marital conflict.

"Financial harmony occurs when spouses are _____, not when they are _____" (p. 67).

In the section titled "The 'I' Word" (p. 68), what is the advanced version of what you felt and experienced back in Stage 1 that is critical for the development of financial harmony in your marriage?

What is the definition of this kind of emotional intimacy?

Is there a neutral zone between emotional distance and emotional intimacy?

Describe the ways that you and your spouse have the characteristics of magnets.

Since we now know it's either one or the other, would you say you and your spouse are currently in attracting or repelling mode?

Does conflict alone twist a relationship so that the partners begin to repel (pp. 69–70)?

What builds barriers that eventually close down communication within a marriage relationship (p. 70)?

What does the text state is the most important thing you can take from chapter 5?

What is the shortcut to intimacy?

What is the precious gift you and your spouse promised each other before God and everyone who witnessed that event on your wedding day?

What are five deep emotional needs every woman desires from her husband and cannot live without?

    1.

    2.

    3.

    4.

    5.

What are five important needs that a man cannot live without and looks to his wife to fulfill?

    1.

    2.

    3.

4.

5.

Dr. Willard Harley, author of a favorite book of mine, *His Needs, Her Needs*, describes a kind of figurative and emotional "bank" that each of us has. What is that specifically, and how would you describe it (p. 72)?

At this time, does your Love Bank show a healthy balance or is it desperately overdrawn? What about your spouse's Love Bank?

What are three ways you can begin today to make investments into your marriage by making deposits into your spouse's Love Bank?

Are you willing to become a regular depositor starting today even though you may not know exactly how to do that?

TO DO

Get two different colored pens, then each of you, using one of them, mark the appropriate box or boxes to the right of each characteristic as you believe it best describes you and your spouse.

We Are So Different!

Characteristic	Him	Her	Both	Neither
Intellectual				
Creative				
Insightful				
Talkative				
Controlling				
Compulsive				
Stubborn				
Morning person				
Night owl				
Expressive				
Introvert				
Extrovert				
Logical				
Emotional				
Good with money				
Terrible with money				
Assertive				
Sensible				
Mechanical				
Self-disciplined				
Funny				
Musical				
Diplomatic				
Reliable				

Pillow Talk

Tell your spouse about three specific things he or she can do to make deposits into your Love Bank.

6

For Wives Only

Okay, girls, think of this as Girl's Night Out. It's just us, and it's time for some serious girl talk.

You've heard it over and again that you cannot change another person—the only person you can change is yourself. That is true, but it is also true that we have tremendous influence over those around us—especially our children and husbands. We can change the outcome of a situation; we can influence the mood of an encounter.

Face it. Most of us female types really like to be in control of things. We have natural born talents when it comes to caretaking and nurturing. It's in our genes! And when these talents are used to manage a household and nurture children, it's great. But our amazing abilities can also become our worst enemy.

There are some who say the woman is the barometer of the home. If she's excited and happy, that's the tone she sets for everyone who comes through the door. If she's depressed and downhearted, it casts a dark shadow over everyone. You've heard it before, "If Mama ain't happy, ain't nobody happy!" You have a tremendous ability to determine the "temperature" within your home. You can use that in a positive way or in a way that is emotionally negative.

"If you know how to push [your husband's] buttons to effect a negative response, you have the power to push his positive buttons to produce positive results" (p. 74).

40

List three things you could do (but of course you don't want to) to make your husband angry and frustrated (p. 76).

Would you say that in general when it comes to your home, your kids, and so on, you have natural abilities to manage, direct, supervise, and coach? Do you feel better when you are in charge of everything and everybody? Describe that.

"The truth is, there's not one controlling behavior that will do anything to change your husband. More likely these behaviors will repel him and push him away so that he withdraws emotionally. And that will leave both of you lonely, unfulfilled, and frustrated" (p. 76).

Now list three specific things you know you can do to evoke a positive result. Remember, every man has a great need to be respected and admired, so anything you can do to convey that message pushes his positive buttons.

Think back to a time that you pushed your husband's buttons in a negative way. What was the result?

If you could have a "do over," what would you do under the same circumstances to effect a positive reaction?

TO DO

For the next two weeks (14 days) keep an ongoing list of things you admire about your husband. These can be characteristics, actions, habits, or attitudes that you observe, respect, and admire. Be sure to write them down and review them often.

Refer to the list of ways wives can show respect for their husbands (pp. 77–78). Imagine for a moment that for ten times in a row you chose to effect a positive reaction (which could be a lot of work if doing the opposite comes more naturally to you). What payoff could you expect?

Do you think that would be worth the effort?

Wedding ceremonies commonly include words like: "Will you have this woman as your lawful wedded wife, to live together in the estate of matrimony? Will you love her, honor her, comfort her, and keep her in sickness and in health; forsaking all others, be true to her as long as you both shall live?" What did "forsaking all others" mean to you then? What does it mean to you now that you have read chapter 6 in the text (p. 74)?

What responsibility does this place on you?

Marriage therapists and authors Gary and Barbara Rosberg say that when our needs are not being met, it's not unusual for men and women alike to become angry because we feel disconnected. That is very scary. It causes us to either retreat or to lash out, which leads to a breakdown of marital communication and intimacy and eventually can pull a couple apart. It's not their differences that come between couples—it's the anger, the pulling away, and the eventual fallout from unfulfilled needs.

Does the Rosbergs' description bring any specific instance from the past to your mind? In what ways could you have changed your response and reaction to preclude your husband pulling away?

Your husband needs you to accept him unconditionally and to always remind him that together you are going to be okay. He doesn't need judgment (there are plenty of people in his life doing that already); he doesn't need criticism. He sure doesn't need rejection, even if in your mind it's so minor it doesn't warrant a second thought. He needs you to accept him, love him, and remind him often that your love is unconditional.

TO DO

In the coming month discover five more ways to answer, "My husband feels loved when . . ." and with that knowledge begin making major deposits into his Love Bank.

Complete the following: My husband feels loved when . . .

1.

2.

3.

As you concentrate on meeting your husband's deepest emotional needs, your husband will see you as the safe harbor, not a place of possible threat. He'll look forward to getting home, not put it off as long as he can.

Become a student of your husband. Know him as a man, as your soul mate, and as your best friend. Know him as your lover, as the person you want to walk through life with, as your partner, your equal, your protector, and your nurturer. Know what concerns him, what makes him feel secure, what gives him intense pleasure, what angers him, and what makes him feel disrespected. Know his dreams and concerns, his likes and his dislikes.

Pillow Talk

Tell your husband about the things that make you happy in your relationship, like having coffee together in the morning. One study showed that couples who did this reduced their stress level by 15 percent. Couples who talk about the things they didn't like about their relationships, however, saw their stress level rise significantly.

7

For Husbands Only

Okay guys, there are a couple of things we need to talk about.

> On your wedding day your wife, the love of your life, made a promise before God and everyone who attended to "forsake all others" and keep herself only unto you. I don't know what you thought when you heard those words, but I know that when I answered, "I will," I thought the minister was referring to sex—a promise to be monogamous. Many years and lot of experience later, I know that our vows were about more than that—a lot more. So were yours. (p. 80)

Speaking of your wife's emotional needs, the most important thing you can know is that just because affection on a daily basis is not necessarily high on your personal list of needs doesn't mean your wife shares that same take-it-or-leave-it attitude. In fact, she has no control over her need for affection because she's genetically predisposed for it.

I am going to assume that as part of your wedding ceremony your wife responded "I will" when asked: "Will you have this man as your lawful wedded husband, to live together in the estate of matrimony? Will you love him, honor him, comfort him, and keep him in sickness and in health; forsaking all others, be true to him as long as you both shall live?"

She promised to forsake all others when it comes to having her deepest emotional needs met. She gave you that exclusive right. It is both your responsibility and your joy to make sure that her needs are fulfilled.

On your wedding day, what did it mean to you when your wife said, "Forsaking all others as long as you both live"?

What does it mean to you now that you have read chapter 6 in the text (p. 74)?

Dr. Willard Harley, author and counselor, says your wife needs and cannot live without affection. It is one of her deepest emotional needs. The kind of affection she needs from you is not sexual. And it is not the same as the affection she might derive from a friend's hug or a birthday card from her father. Every day she needs words, gestures, and actions from you that convey specific messages like, "You are more important to me than any other person on earth."

Generally speaking, affection to a woman is words, gestures, and actions that convey certain important messages, one of which is: You are important to me (p. 82). There are five other messages your affection conveys as well. What are they?

1.

2.

3.

4.

5.

Okay, so let's say you really do a number on your wife's birthday. You get her a beautiful gift, wrap it well, and top it with a mushy card. How many days' (weeks' or months') worth of affection should a gesture of this magnitude count for? If you do not know for sure, the answer is on page 83.

Daily deposits into your wife's Love Bank in the form of affection is going to have a positive effect on her that will be key to the development of financial harmony in your marriage. What is that effect?

The more affection you give your wife on a daily basis without expectation of anything in return, the more _____ she will give you. But wait! There's more. She'll stop trying to do something else. What is it?

To count as a deposit into her Love Bank, your affection must be:

1. verbal
2. nonverbal
3. both verbal and nonverbal

TO DO

Tonight, tell your wife to find something else to do because you are going to do the dishes. Couples who share housework duties report they are 19 percent more satisfied in their relationship than spouses where one partner does the vast majority of the work. It is also a grand display of affection worthy of several love units.

Having read this chapter, would you say that for your wife quality or quantity of affection is more important?

On page 84 of the text is a list of ways you can make deposits into your wife's Love Bank. Women, as you may have discovered on your own by now, are not all alike. We're similar but still unique. You may have read that list and noticed immediately that what matters most to your wife isn't there! Well now's your chance to expand that list. Do it right here, being as specific as possible.

Below, list again your wife's Top Five Deep Emotional Needs, of which affection is #1. If you need a memory jogger, refer to page 71 of the text.

1.

2.

3.

4.

5.

There's no doubt that a successful relationship is a lot of work. But I can assure you that the payoff in terms of mutual satisfaction and harmony will be immeasurable.

Pillow Talk

Your assignment is to discover five new ways to give your wife her daily dose of affection. Asking for her input is not cheating and is in fact an excellent idea.

8

Getting It Together

I thoroughly enjoy jigsaw puzzles. But I have to admit I'm not wild about that starting part. I like to come in when the edges are in place and someone else has done a lot of the grunt work. Once I can see it taking form, I'm very enthusiastic. I just don't care for that part that includes dumping the pieces from the box, tediously turning all of them face up, searching for those key starting pieces. You are not likely to catch me starting a puzzle from scratch.

Before you started this work, you might have felt your finances were the monetary equivalent of a 10,000-piece jigsaw puzzle.

Now slowly, one chapter, one question, one page at a time, you've begun to turn the pieces face up, so you can see where you are and the scope of the task. You've been doing the equivalent of staring at the finished photo on the box cover. You are starting to see that we really are headed someplace; there truly is a method in all of this. With chapter 8, we begin to put the pieces together.

What two ingredients are necessary to create emotional intimacy in your marriage?

What is the "self-perpetuating" cycle?

Which best describes the way you have handled finances in your marriage in the past?

1. Equal. We both know what's going on and participate together in paying bills and making financial decisions.
2. He makes the money; it's her job to manage it.
3. He makes and manages the money; her job is to take care of the kids and the house.
4. Other:
5. None of the above; we cannot even fill in "other" because it's so haphazard and so out of whack, it defies description.

Have you ever owned a business or been a business partner? If so, did you ever have the luxury of not having to carry any of the responsibility of the day-to-day business but instead grabbed a big fat paycheck without having any responsibilities? Explain.

What do studies show regarding married people who behave in their marriages as true financial partners?

Why do you think that happens?

In your own words, describe the five characteristics of financial partners.

1.

2.

3.

4.

5.

How many "hats" would you say you wear in your regular routine of life (pp. 86–87)? List them here.

On page 87 is an illustration of how a simple business partnership works. Using this model as your guide, describe how the business-like partnership might work within your marriage.

"Time to Talk." On the off chance you need some idea starters for your fifteen minutes of daily meaningful uninterrupted and distraction-free conversation (p. 87), I offer the following list. It's designed to help you get to know one another better through conversation. These are not presented for your written answers but rather to be used during your talk time.

1. My three best attributes. Tell each other what you like the most about yourself—your best characteristics and qualities.
2. My three worst attributes. The areas you think you need to work on.
3. On a scale of one to ten (with one being the least intelligent and ten being the most), when I think of my intelligence I think I'm a ____.
4. On a scale of one to ten (with one being the least attractive, ten being the most attractive), when I think of my attractiveness I think I'm a ____.
5. On a scale of one to ten (with one being very shy and ten very outgoing), rate your social competence.
6. Rate yourself on the one to ten scale for artistic ability and creativity.
7. If I could change one thing about myself, it would be:
8. Two things that make me feel like I look great are:
9. Two things that make me feel terrific about myself are:
10. Two things that make me feel cared about are:
11. My current biggest fear is:
12. My secret dream at this moment is:
13. The one thing I need the most right now is:
14. My biggest pet peeve is:
15. My biggest financial concern right now is:
16. The worst habit I have and wish I could break is:
17. The person who has influenced me most in my life is _____. Why?
18. My greatest regret in the past year, and the greatest joy in my life:
19. My greatest achievements are:
20. When and where I am the happiest (the time and place where you feel everything is just as it should be):
21. The three things that are most important to me are:

22. Three things I hope to accomplish or complete in the next three months are:
23. Something I'd like to accomplish before I die is:
24. Three things I need my spouse's help to accomplish are:
25. The thing I most value in a friend is:
26. Three things I would do if I only had the time are:
27. Three things I would do if I had the money are:
28. The three defining concepts of my spiritual life (what I believe) are:
29. The person I consider to be my best friend is:
30. Three things I really like about our home are:
31. Three things I would like to change about our home are:
32. My least favorite household chore is:
33. Two things that make me happiest about our family are:
34. Two things that make me proudest about my spouse are:

Good conversation doesn't just happen; it takes work. The three fundamentals of effective communication are:

1. good eye contact
2. one speaker
3. one listener

A good speaker gives his or her views, stating the facts and also expressing his or her feelings. Be specific, positive, and stay away from using the words "never" and "always."

A good listener respects the speaker's moment, listens intently, doesn't interrupt with questions, doesn't respond with his or her own opinion, and doesn't make suggestions. And the most difficult task for listeners: Do not make judgments. This is not a trial.

Once you've both spoken on a particular topic or question, discuss it briefly and nonjudgmentally, trying to stick to the one speaker, one listener rule.

Let's say you need to talk about some pressing issue and your first inclination is to start fighting about it. Describe how you should go about talking without fighting (p. 88).

What is "brainstorming," where did it originate, and how could this communication technique work in your marriage? Give one or two specific examples or topics.

Talking with your spouse is probably the best way to tear down barriers that have built up in the past. According to one study, what percentage of all conflicts in marriage resolve themselves by simply talking about them (p. 90)?

Decisions made in haste often lead to what end?

Pillow Talk

Decide the time and place for your first time-to-talk. Share your misgivings, fears, or hesitations. It can be threatening to share those parts of your heart you've never shared before. Give your spouse the assurance that your desire is to become a safe and soft place to fall.

Part 2

How to Debt-Proof Your Marriage

9

Debt-Proof Living

Perhaps your finances are in shambles and you cannot wait to get everything back on track, or you have your money completely under control and are looking for ways to do even better. Or, more likely, you find yourselves somewhere between those two extremes. The point is that we all have room to improve the way that we manage our money and plan for the future. So no matter your current situation, you can expect better days are ahead.

In the space below, write a brief assessment from your perspective of your current financial situation followed by what you hope to gain from learning how to debt-proof your marriage.

He says:

She says:

Each of you place a check mark beside every statement that describes how you are feeling about your financial situation.

1. It's too late; nothing can help us now.
2. I'm willing to try again. But we've failed so many times in the past, I am not optimistic that this will work.
3. We didn't get into this mess overnight, so it's going to take time. But we've got time and we've got each other.
4. I'll give it my best shot; that's the best I can do.
5. I am totally committed to doing whatever is necessary to getting out of debt and living within our means.
6. This is going to work; it has to work. We have no other option but to make sure it does work.

What is the difference between a principle-based money management system and an emotionally based method (pp. 93–94)?

List several reasons why it is important that your money management not be based on feelings and emotions.

The last reported median income for a family of four in the U.S. is $62,228. Yours may be higher or lower. In the space below, write the figure which is your combined annual income. Multiply by the number of years you intend to work into the future.

$_____ X _____ years = $_____

That last figure is the amount of money you can expect to manage from now until you retire. This doesn't mean you won't have money to manage after retirement, but it does give quite a wake-up call, doesn't it? Factor in pay increases, and the number only gets higher. Perhaps your dreams of having a lot of money have already been realized and you did not recognize it.

Reread pages 93–95 in the text. Discuss and then come up with one answer between the two of you for this question: What does it mean to you as a couple to debt-proof your marriage? Write your answer below.

What grade would each of you give your high school for how well it prepared you to manage your personal finances? She: _____ He: _____

Why do you need to debt-proof your marriage? Place the numbers one through five next to the reasons below so that one is next to the reason which is most important to you right now and five is next to the least.

_____ To insure our marriage
_____ To survive lean times
_____ To reduce our stress
_____ To teach our children
_____ To allow God to care for us

How do you personally distinguish a "need" from a "want," and when is it appropriate to fulfill your wants?

She says:

He says:

TO DO

Put on a favorite CD or tape. Studies show that when couples listen to music they both like, they feel more cooperative and caring toward their spouse. Why? Music dissipates tension and puts both of you in a good mood.

In your own words and in the spaces below, summarize each of the Debt-Proof Principles (pp. 97–100). Make them personal. If you take issue with them in any way, now is the time to discuss that and to come to a meeting of your minds so that you can embrace these principles as a team. Negotiate, compromise, and work at it until you can agree completely.

Principle #1: God is the source.

Principle #2: Money is not for spending.

Principle #3: Never keep it all.

Principle #4: Never spend it all.

Principle #5: No more new debt.

Principle #6: More money is not the solution.

Pillow Talk

You read about the famous "cables" on Half-Dome in Yosemite National Park (p. 97). Your journey together through life has likely had its difficult times and steep climbs. Tell your spouse how much you count on him/her to pull you up when the going gets tough.

10

Till Debt Do Us Part

There's nothing like a big load of debt to put a major strain on a marriage. Americans owe an average of $8,940 per household in credit card debt alone. That doesn't count mortgages, home equity loans (HELs), auto loans, or student debt. Still that figure is up 8.5 percent from 2001 and a big fat whopping 178 percent from 1992.

You met Spike Retherford on page 102. He gets preapproved credit card offers all the time. I get them, and I'll bet you get those annoying pieces of junk mail too. What makes Spike any different than the rest of us?

You've likely heard of similar credit card atrocities, like a college freshman without a job or parental approval snatching up five or six cards while waiting in line to register for classes and racking up $25,000 of debt before the end of the first semester. Actually that young man and I were on the same TV show, and did he ever have some entitlement issues!

Describe below the most ridiculous credit card story you've heard of involving a child, a pet, or an adult acting like a child.

All debt can be divided into two categories. What are they?

    1.

    2.

What are the basic characteristics of "intelligent borrowing," also known as "secured debt" (pp. 103–104)?

    1.

    2.

    3.

    4.

    5.

Now compare unsecured debt or "stupid debt" with those characteristics (p. 104):

What are the five probing questions you should ask to determine if a loan would produce stupid debt (p. 105)?

Credit card issuers rely heavily on the interest they collect from their customers who carry revolving balances. But that's not the only or even the largest source of their revenue. From what consumer activities do credit card issuers derive approximately 30 percent of their profits?

What is the average credit card annual interest rate? _____

What is a "semistupid" debt? What makes a debt "somewhat intelligent" (pp. 106–108)?

TO DO

Without spending a lot of time, list the loans and debts you've incurred and carried during your marriage to the present. Indicate which of them were/are *secured* or *unsecured*. Place a star next to those that have been paid in full. Estimate how much you've paid just in interest on those debts.

Pillow Talk

Debt takes away our options. It turns over control of where we will spend our money to creditors. Maybe debt makes you feel trapped in a job you don't like but cannot afford to leave. Talk with your spouse about the options you feel you have lost because of your debt and how your lives will change when you pay off debt and get those options back.

II

You Are Here

Ever been lost? Perhaps it happened when you were just a young child, or maybe it was last week when you couldn't find your car in the mall parking lot. Describe that event and the fear you suffered that you would never be found or find your own way out.

She says:

He says:

Being lost physically has many parallels to feeling lost financially. The panic, fear, and uncertainty are very similar. And discovering your way out of both situations can be similarly exhilarating.

It is always good to know where you are, whether you are trekking through the forest or facing your financial condition. I'm not saying that finding your way through your financial situation is going to be particularly enjoyable, but it's something that you must do. Figuring out your finances can be intimidating, particularly when you are deeply in debt and may be assuming the worst. But this is something you must do, and now is the time.

Take a look at the illustrations on pages 110–11 of the text. In the space below, using two different colors of ink, draw a general picture of your income vs. expenses since you were married. This is not meant to be exact, so don't struggle. However, if you are deeply in debt now, "Your Spending" will be higher than "Your Income."

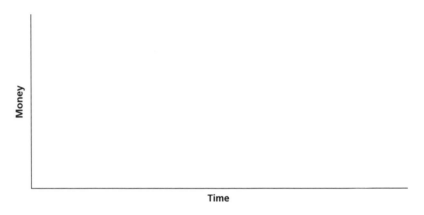

Now, in the next space, draw the graph the way it would appear if you could go back to day one and start over:

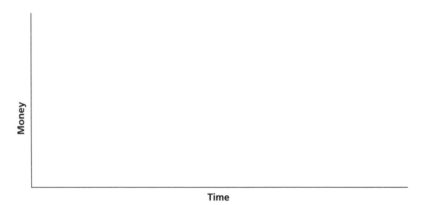

What is a Balance Sheet (p. 114)?

It is sometimes referred to by a different name. What is that?

Basically your Balance Sheet will reveal three things:

1. What you own (_____).
2. What you owe (_____).
3. Your Net Worth, which is the difference.

What are the six things your Balance Sheet will do for you?

1.

2.

3.

4.

5.

6.

As you face this task of preparing your Balance Sheet, what, if any, fears are you experiencing? Why does this task of creating your Balance Sheet make you uneasy?

What do you gain by remaining in denial, hoping everything will work out somehow in the future?

Balance Sheet

Net Worth as of _____

Wealth-Building Assets
_____

Cash
_____

_____ $_____

_____ _____

_____ _____

_____ _____

_____ _____

_____ _____

Other Assets
_____

_____ $_____

_____ _____

_____ _____

_____ _____

_____ _____

_____ _____

Total Assets $_____

Liabilities
_____

_____ $_____

_____ _____

_____ _____

_____ _____

_____ _____

_____ _____

_____ _____

Total Liabilities $_____

Net Worth
(Total Assets Less Total Liabilities) $_____

What is a "Wealth-Building" Asset (p. 117)?

What are "Other Assets" and why are they put in a separate category under "Assets"?

What are "Liabilities" as it pertains to your Balance Sheet?

Look at one of your liabilities. If you were to reduce it by $100 tomorrow, how would that effort affect your Net Worth (p. 120)?

What does it mean to be "in the red" (p. 119)?

Referring to your newly completed Balance Sheet, may I be the first to say, "Congratulations." You faced the reality of your current financial situation. Sure you can continue to run and hide and pretend that it doesn't matter how much you spend or what you do with your money. You can continue to assume that the only thing that matters is if you can keep the bills current or how much more credit you can amass. Or you can face the truth, get real about the way money is leaking out of your life, and make a decision right now to do something about it.

Starting today, what are five things you can do to improve your Net Worth?

1.

2.

3.

4.

5.

TO DO

Now that you've spent the time and energy to find your important papers and figure out your assets and liabilities, determine the safe place you will keep these documents. File them carefully along with a copy of the Balance Sheet you have just completed. Now schedule a date six months or a year from now when you will complete another Balance Sheet. It will be interesting to compare your Net Worth at that time with the statement you have just completed.

Pillow Talk

Net Worth is important because it measures the extent to which you have been responsible stewards of the resources you've been given to manage. But Net Worth cannot hold a candle to deep, meaningful and romantic love. Tell your spouse how much his/her worth is greater than any material possession or bank account.

12

Getting to Where You Want to Be

I have never been involved directly in building a house. However, I understand from those who have that the planning and preparation phase of the project can be long and agonizing.

The site must be prepared, and that can include demolition and clean up of the land. Depending on the location, geology reports may be required and work done to fix soil problems. Then there's the small matter of transferring the homeowner-to-be's dreams and vision of the house to the mind and pen of an architect. Once the plans meet the approval of all involved, from the people down at the City Planning and Zoning Department to the people who will be living in this dream house, the search begins for a builder and subcontractors and landscape designers and decorators.

While it may look to outsiders as if the property has been abandoned—that the owners have changed their minds about building—the truth is the most important work has been going on behind the scenes.

Up to this time in this matter of debt-proofing your marriage, you've been doing the work of preparation and planning. You've been assessing your relationship, improving your emotional intimacy, figuring out where you are financially, and learning what it means to debt-proof your marriage. Everything is now in place. You are ready to break ground. Let the construction begin!

"The debt-proof plan consists of a formula and four tangible elements that you will be able to hold in your hands" (p. 126). Briefly describe them.

The Formula:

Element #1:

Element #2:

Element #3:

Element #4:

Creating your unique money management plan is a lot like building a house. Your "house" will have the same infrastructure and be the same as all other couples' financial plans built on the debt-proof model. Will this be true for the long-term?

A plan to get out of debt is one thing, but with the understanding you have at this time, will you need a new money management plan once you are out of debt and as your financial picture changes and improves in the future (p. 126)?

Describe the feeling you have now that you know you are about to break ground on a plan that has the potential to change your lives. Are you giddy with excitement, weighed down with skepticism, or more like I'll-believe-it-when-I-see-it?

She says:

He says:

Pillow Talk

You've read the debt-proof living Formula. It provides that you give away part of your income. Are you (1) shocked because you don't have enough money as it is so how can you give any away, (2) relieved because in your heart you've always known that is what you should be doing, or (3) is it something between? Share how you really feel about this with your financial partner.

13

A Life-Changing Formula

If you are carrying unsecured debts in the form of credit card balances, student debt, and other types of "signature" loans, you are living beyond your means. You are unable to support the lifestyle you have chosen even while using 100 percent of your income.

If you can't make it on 100 percent, you may be wondering what kind of a fool would suggest you could do better on even less? I would be that fool (it's okay, I get this a lot). The truth of the matter is if you're carrying a load of debt, you are probably living on something closer to 125 percent of your income, and that is a real problem, as you may have already discovered. Worse, you probably don't know for sure where all your money goes or how much your current lifestyle actually costs. That's a real problem. And I believe I have the solution.

To what era can we trace the 10-10-80 formula?

Describe in your own words what the 10-10-80 formula means (p. 130).

Compare the principles of the 10-10-80 formula with the way you've been managing—or failing to manage—your money up until now.

She says:

He says:

Why give? List five reasons you need to become givers. Explain each.

   1.

   2.

   3.

   4.

   5.

What questions should you ask yourselves as you make a decision for the place you will give?

Fill in the blanks for this short passage taken from page 131 of the text:
"As long as you are giving with _____ _____ attached and no
_____ of anything in return, you can make just
about _____ or _____ the object
of your giving." However, there are several things to keep in mind. What are
they?

    1.

    2.

    3.

The text gives basic guidelines on how to set up a giving program. What
are they (pp. 131–32)?

"Your willingness and commitment to giving back some of what is so precious to you (your money) proves the condition of your hearts. More than
anything else, God is concerned about the condition of your hearts" (p. 132).
What is your reaction to that statement, and how would you assess the condition of your heart right now?
    She says:

    He says:

What is the meaning of the second "10" in the 10-10-80 formula?

TO DO

Locate a copy of *The Richest Man in Babylon* by George S. Clason (Signet, re-issued in 2002, $6.99) either in the library or bookstore. It's a small paperback, just 160 pages. Read and enjoy it together.

Do you find it odd or perhaps wrong to keep some of your money for yourselves while you owe so much to so many? Or are you amazed at the prospect and almost feel that someone has given you permission to do something you assumed was unethical or dishonest?

She says:

He says:

What will a consistent savings program do for your self-worth (p. 133)?

What else will saving money do for you and your marriage?

Seeing yourselves as worthy enough to keep some of the money you have been given the responsibility to manage is going to be key in fixing your money ills. Saving money is going to change your attitude and give you the courage and the strength to face the challenges that lie ahead. Saving money is one of the best attitude adjusters you will ever know. And since debt-proofing your marriage is going to be 10 percent about money and 90 percent about your attitude, you cannot get started soon enough. (p. 133)

I wish I could require you to write the preceding paragraph on the chalkboard one thousand times. But alas, that's just not possible. Instead, copy that paragraph below, and as you write the words, meditate on them. Read them aloud, recite them to each other, plant them in your heart, and let them bind you together in your resolve and your commitment. Let their spark ignite your commitment and optimism for what is ahead.

What is the correlation between saving and seatbelts?

Have you ever experienced what some call "shopper's high"? If yes, describe it. If not, describe what you think it might be—or if you think it's a myth, you can say that too.

She says:

He says:

What gives the same satisfaction as spending with plastic but doesn't wear off?

"Giving to others and saving for the future puts things into proper perspective, and that's when I find contentment. I understand that I am not in charge of my life, that I am a steward, a caretaker to whom God has entrusted a portion of his abundance. And when he sees that he can trust us with those gifts, I believe that pleases him, and then he can trust us with more" (p. 134). Do you concur, disagree, or is this so new you haven't had time to digest such an amazing thought? Explain.

She says:

He says:

What are some of the other ways that giving and saving can impact your life for the good?

Briefly explain the 80 Percent Solution (p. 135).

What is your first reaction to the idea that someone might use the words "frugal," "thrifty," or "cheap" to describe you? How or with whom have you associated those words in the past?

What does "frugality" really mean (p. 135)?

How would you explain the term "living below your means"?

Does this give you a new attitude about the matter of frugality? If yes, describe that now.

Pillow Talk

You either embraced the money style of your parents or rebelled against it. Share with your spouse your perception of the environment you grew up in. Were your parents "frugal" and you turned out that way too, or were they "frugal" and you did everything you could to make sure you never repeated that way of life? Or were they spendthrifts and you grew up knowing you never wanted to live like that?

14

Knowledge Is a Powerful Thing

"For me the word 'budget' is like fingernails on a chalkboard. It screeches confinement, deprivation. Like a straitjacket. Or worse, a diet!" (p. 137). How does that word affect you?

Have you ever been on a budget in the past? If so, how did that work out for you?

List three characteristics of a "budget."

1.

2.

3.

Now give three characteristics of a "Spending Plan."

1.

2.

3.

Briefly make the analogy between an architect and a Spending Plan (p. 137).

If you have read chapters 14–18 in *Debt-Proof Your Marriage*, you know that creating your Spending Plan is the big task we're about to undertake. If you haven't read it, then I'm telling you this now. It's a big job, a multistep process. And we're going to do it together, step by step.

If you're at all like me, you like to know where we're going and how we're going to get there. Commencing with this chapter, my goal is to help you create your unique Monthly Spending Plan that will work for you in the coming month and for every month thereafter. That's where we're going, and we'll land there in chapter 18. And here is how we're going to get there.

In this chapter you will learn how to track your spending and then use that information to create a Monthly Spending Record—a single sheet of paper that shows you where all of your money goes. This is information we will need for your Spending Plan in chapter 18.

In chapter 15 you will learn what to do with that 10 percent of your income you will begin saving. You will be developing your Contingency Fund. This is another vital piece of information you will need to create your Spending Plan in chapter 18.

Chapter 16 will be Freedom Account time, and what an amazing thing this is going to be. I don't want to spoil all the fun now, but suffice it to say that your Freedom Account will be yet another vital puzzle piece you will need to create your Spending Plan in chapter 18.

Chapter 17 will be my chance to show you something absolutely amazing—how you are going to get out of debt. And let me tell you that you are going to love this, so just get ready to be amazed. Your Rapid Debt-Repayment Plan will be the last important piece of the Spending Plan puzzle.

And that, my friends, will take us directly to chapter 18, where we will take your Spending Record, Contingency Fund, Freedom Account, and Rapid Debt-Repayment Plan and put together your unique and life-changing Spending Plan.

I tell you this because I don't want to leave you hanging when we get to the end of this chapter (14) and all you have is homework and nothing close to the Spending Plan, which I mentioned at the outset of this chapter.

Okay, I've been rattling on long enough. It's your turn. What are the four key elements, or pieces, of information you will need to create your Spending Plan?

1.

2.

3.

4.

We are now in chapter 14. In which chapter will we actually create your Spending Plan?

What are the two vitally important pieces of information you need to get started on this quest to create your Spending Plan (p. 139)?

1.

2.

If you do not have this information readily available, do you think you are *unusual* or *typical* as compared to a cross section of married couples?

_____

Based on my personal experience, as well as what I've learned from so many other couples like you, I would say that if you don't have a good handle on your average monthly net income without doing a lot of figuring and even less knowledge on exactly where that money goes, you are typical. But not for long! My goal is to make you odd. Ha, ha. Okay, back to work:

Using your best information, a calculator, and the information on page 140, figure your average monthly household income in the space below. Only include sources of income that you can reasonably count on. For example, if one of you is supposed to receive court-mandated child support, but you haven't seen a payment for a very long time, don't count that. If you sometimes work overtime but do not have any guarantee that you will in the future, do not count on that. If you are sure you'll be heir to a fortune someday, well that's great, and I hope you're right, but you cannot count on that now. If, on the other hand, since the day you were born, your great aunt Hildegard has sent you a check for $10,000 on your birthday and she is in fairly good health, go ahead. Count it.

Work Space:

Our average monthly income as of _____ is $_____
_____.

Is this about what you figured? Higher, lower?
She says:

He says:

Okay, there you have the first piece of information you will need to develop your Spending Plan in chapter 18. So it's onward and upward.

Now that you know how much you bring in, you need to determine what happens to it. I don't mean just the big chunks. You know about the rent or mortgage payment, but what about all the little stuff? Where *does* your money go?

> If there were any way possible for you reconstruct your spending over the past few months so you could see where all of your money goes, that's exactly what I would ask you to do. But if you haven't been recording that all along, it will be impossible. Sure, you can come up with the big things like rent, mortgage payments, and other items for which you have a paper trail of cancelled checks and account statements. But as big and important as those expenses are, they alone do not give an accurate account of what happened to your money. The only way to find out is to begin tracking now. (p. 141)

I'm going to assume both of you are able to track your spending. But are you both ready and willing?

She says:

He says:

Reread "Where Does It Go?" on page 141 and "Daily Spending" on page 142, and meet me back here when you're done.

As you anticipate keeping Daily Spending Records for the next thirty days and given your lifestyle and current life situation, how do you predict this effort is going to rate on your Hassle Meter where one is "No Problem" and ten is "A Royal Pain"? Write your answer below.

She says:

He says:

Don't underestimate what kind of an adjustment keeping track of your daily expenditures is going to require. You've been conditioned for many years to not think about your spending and to grab all of the convenience possible so you can avoid doing the very thing I am now advocating: thinking about where all your money goes. It's only my suggestion, but I think you would be well advised to anticipate a "five" on the Hassle Meter. This way when it is a challenge, you will not be tempted to throw the book at me and go back to your old ways. And when it turns out to be a lot less hassle than you anticipated, you'll be my friend for life. Right?

TO DO

Decide how each of you will manage recording your Daily Spending. You'll each need something handy to write on and a plan for where you will keep your list during the day (pocket, purse . . . that kind of thing) and where both of you will deposit your records at the end of each day. Make a plan and keep it simple.

Referring to what you just read, what is the purpose of keeping track of your spending?

Do you see yourselves as being in a kind of financial fog? Explain.

The minimum time required to start clearing that fog is thirty days. While you can start any time, it is important that you track for one full _____ _____ (p. 142).

In the debt-proof method, every month is the same without regard to the days of the week. Explain this by filling in the blanks below:

Week 1 is always days _____ through _____.
Week 2 is always days _____ through _____.
Week 3 is always days _____ through _____.
Week 4 is always days _____ through _____.

What kind of a problem is it going to create when the fourth week in the month has more than seven days? _____

Which types of expenditures should you record on your Daily Spending Record?

1. Cash purchases
2. Debit card transactions
3. Credit card transactions
4. Checks I write
5. All of the above

In that I don't want to bother you with a secret answer sheet at the end of the book, I'll give you the answers as we go (I'm such a pushover). The answer to the above question is, of course—all of the above. Remember, this is in addition to any recording you do otherwise. You should still record your checks in your checkbook register. You should still record your ATM withdrawals (I discovered an easy way to never forget to record one of those. Cut up your ATM card. Really makes spending a hassle, but isn't that the way it should be?).

Take a look at Sally's Daily Spending Record on page 143. Simple, easy. No addition . . . she wrote down two things for each spending opportunity: What and how much?

Okay. It's time. Both of you. Go! I'll meet you back here tomorrow night to see how you did on your first day.

[Passing of time . . .]

Write below how your first day went. Did you forget to record an expenditure? Did you feel awkward or like you're being punished? Or did you find yourself looking for ways not to spend just so you could avoid the hassle? Take a few minutes to record your experiences.

She says:

He says:

Now put today's records away and get ready for tomorrow. Come back at the end of the seventh day, together with all fourteen of your Daily Spending Records.

[More passing of time . . .]

Okay, it's time to gather your Daily Spending Records for one full week and develop them into a Weekly Spending Record. You can use the form that follows (make copies so you'll have plenty for the future). Spread all of your records out and start categorizing. Group like expenditures together, so you come up with one total for the week in each of a number of specific categories. Use Bob and Sally's Weekly Spending Record as a guide (page 146). Don't get too specific, or you'll have such a mess you won't know what to do. But don't be too vague either—you know, two categories: Food and Miscellaneous. That's not going to work!

Common categories might be food, housing, insurance, gasoline, car payments, medical, and so on. Seriously, let me caution you to not put too many things in Miscellaneous or you won't have a good picture of your situation.

Your assignment is to keep going. Keep tracking every day, stashing your Daily Spending Records, turning them into Weekly Spending Records at the end of each week, until you have four weeks . . . one full calendar month.

Now you will need to blend the four Weekly Spending Records into one Monthly Spending Record. You can figure this out . . . you may need to adjust your categories, but keep working with it. Use Bob and Sally's Monthly Spending Record as your model (p. 148).

Once you have all of your figures on the Monthly Spending Record form, total across, and then make one grand spending total for the entire month. Bring that figure to the bottom, and deduct it from your income figure. Surprised? Shocked? Below, write a summary of the facts and your reaction to what you have learned.

She says:

He says:

Has this work of recording your spending been easier, about what you expected, or more difficult than you could have imagined? Explain.

She says:

He says:

No matter how things turned out this month, you deserve congratulations for having stuck with it. I can promise that it will get easier.

Whether you've already gone ahead to the next chapters or held up to work just on this chapter for a full month, it's time to move on. There is so much you need to learn and to incorporate into your collection of puzzle pieces for the eventual Monthly Spending Plan (chapter 18).

In the coming month, unlike in the past, I want you to begin to concentrate on your spending. While recording each expenditure has its own way of making you think about how much you are spending, from now on I want you to not only think about it but question and challenge every expenditure. Especially if your spending went over last month's income. Even if you did not overspend your income, it's possible you didn't give or save; perhaps you put nothing away for irregular expenses. So there's lots of work to do.

Your assignment for the coming month:

1. Continue daily tracking and preparing your Daily, Weekly, and Monthly Records.
2. Be on the lookout for places where money is leaking from your life (hint: fast food!). Think of ways you can "plug" those leaks and keep more of your money.
3. Do not get discouraged. No matter how you are doing, chances are it's 100 percent better than two months ago! If you are holding out for perfection, it's not going to happen, so be grateful for the progress and just keep going.

Now that you have done Daily, Weekly, and Monthly Spending Records, I have something to tell you, which I would not have told you in the beginning. The step you have just completed is by far the most difficult part of my entire debt-proof living plan. But you did it! So here's a high-five for both of you.

Pillow Talk

Tell each other how it really feels to be taking this bold move of keeping written records of your spending. Don't be surprised if this is a bigger issue for you than for your spouse. Talk about issues of accountability and privacy—of having something so personal as your daily spending exposed so openly. If you are uncomfortable or feeling threatened, admit it. As difficult as this work is, express your gratitude for having taken the brave move to begin to clear your financial fog.

Weekly Spending Record

Month_____ Week # _____

Category	Amount

Total _____

Monthly Spending Record

Month: _____

Category	Week 1 1–7	Week 2 8–15	Week 3 16–21	Week 4 22–End	Actually Spent
_____					
_____					
_____					
_____					
_____					
_____					
_____					
_____					
_____					
_____					
_____					
_____					
_____					
_____					
_____					
_____					
_____					
_____					
Totals					

15

You Want Security?
I'll Show You Security!

Have you ever been on the edge? You will recall from chapter 1 that I've been there once or twice myself. As long as I live I will never forget what it was like to lose our business, have absolutely no income (not even a pitiful unemployment check), no savings, no available credit, and nothing on the horizon—just mountains of debt, angry creditors, and a foreclosure-happy mortgage lender. We were literally pinned against the wall with no wiggle room at all. There is no way I could adequately describe what that was like. Any attempt would include words like pain, desperation, anxiety, fear, and worry. A physical demonstration would require a pair of vice grips clamped to my stomach and twisted as tightly as possible. Finally I'd have to turn out the lights because life on the edge can be a very dark and lonely place.

Have you ever been on the edge, financially speaking? If so, what were the circumstances? If not, imagine what that might be like.

He says:

She says:

94

No matter your season of life, your income level, financial situation, stage of marriage or age, for debt-proof living to work you must have a Contingency Fund—that's one Contingency Fund per household. I just don't know any way to make that any clearer.

What is a Contingency Fund?

What is it for?

Who needs a Contingency Fund and why?

What effect do you think building and maintaining a Contingency Fund will have on your marriage?

How much money does it take to establish a Contingency Fund?

You will begin making regular deposits to your Contingency Fund. "Contingency Fund" will become a standard category on your Monthly Spending Plan (chapter 18). Keeping the 10-10-80 formula in mind, where will your Contingency Fund deposits come from?

What are the three factors to consider when selecting a parking place for your Contingency Fund?

Let's say your gross income is $5,000 a month. However, by the time you allow for taxes and other deductions plus work-related expenses you would not have during a time of unemployment, you could probably get by on $3,200 or less. In this example, your Contingency Fund goal would be $3,200 times three, or $9,600 at the least. Multiply by six to get the maximum savings goal of $19,200. Shocked? Take a deep breath and slowly exhale. There, you'll be okay. Reality can be daunting, especially if you, like the majority of Americans, have something like $1.32 in savings.

Generally speaking, your Contingency Fund needs to have a balance equal to your minimum monthly requirements times three . . . six is better. Figure that below:

$_____ x 3 = $_____

$_____ x 6 = $_____

If that's too much to handle right now, let's break this down even further. Divide your average monthly net income by thirty.

$_____ ÷ 30 = $_____

Start with the goal in mind to build your Contingency Fund to cover one day without a paycheck. Then multiply that by seven and head for a week. Soon you'll reach one month's income in your Contingency Fund.

What are your initial thoughts and reactions when you think about saving a minimum of $10,000? Is it empowering, terrifying, or something in between? Explain.

Imagine for a moment that your Contingency Fund is fully funded with six months of living expenses or $20,000. How does that make you feel?

The Contingency Fund covers the costs related to a "major life event." What for you qualifies as a major life event? (Hint: This response should not contain the words "Nordstrom's Half-Yearly Sale" or "Harley.")

TO DO

Starting a Contingency Fund is simple. Find an envelope, any envelope will do . . . even one of the pre-addressed, postage-paid ones that come in junk mail. Reach into your wallet or purse and pull out a $1 bill. Place said $1 bill into envelope. Write on the front: Contingency Fund. You have just established your Contingency Fund. Begin feeding it now and when it reaches $50, use it to open a savings account at your bank or credit union.

Why doesn't a 401(k) or other retirement fund qualify for your Contingency Fund?

What fringe benefits do you expect to enjoy as a result of starting and building your Contingency Fund?

One of my *Cheapskate Monthly* subscribers found herself suddenly unemployed with $8,200 in her Contingency Fund. She wrote, "One benefit of the Contingency Fund that most folks don't think of is the absence of panic that makes it so much easier to deal with life as it happens."

On page 159 of *Debt-Proof Your Marriage* are two charts, the first shows how long it will take you to save $10,000 in an account earning 4 percent interest, the second 6 percent (those days will return). Given the amount you will be adding to your Contingency Fund each month, how long will it take you to accumulate $10,000?

What specific steps have you taken already or will you take this month to begin building your Contingency Fund?

How does the requirement to save (eventually 10 percent of your income in your Contingency Fund) leave you feeling? Are you terrified, excited, relieved, hopeful, panic-stricken, or other? Explain.

Pillow Talk

Tell your spouse what it would do to your peace of mind and feelings of security to know you would be okay in the event of a sudden job-loss. It is likely that one of you is not as enthusiastic about saving because you have so many needs and your situation is already so tight. Negotiate and compromise until you can agree on a set amount to save each payday and also the total amount in the Contingency Fund.

16

You Want Freedom?
I'll Show You Freedom!

Before the introduction of easy credit, people had no choice but to plan ahead. Failure to anticipate meant certain doom. Our grandparents called it a rainy day, and they were forever putting money away for it—just in case.

Then something happened. The advent of easy consumer credit sent a message telling us that we didn't have to worry anymore about what might happen. Grandpa had his nest egg; we have lines of credit.

Credit companies promised us that as long as we had credit it was impossible to run out of money. Don't worry, they told us! That's what credit cards are for—to be there just in case of emergencies. *Don't think about tomorrow, don't anticipate the future. Go ahead and spend all you have now, and let Master-Card and Visa take care of the rest.*

If you are carrying a load of unsecured consumer debt, I can nearly guarantee that a great portion of it, if not all, is the result of you believing that you don't need to anticipate unexpected expenses and financial emergencies.

What was the reason that you got your first credit card?

1. To have just in case of emergencies
2. I figured if I qualified, I could afford it.
3. To establish credit
4. All of the above

In this chapter, you are going to learn how to create your Freedom Account, which will help you anticipate and prepare for unexpected, irregular, and intermittent expenses.

Think back over the last months or year. Name five unexpected expenses you had that gave you no choice but to pay for them with credit. You called them emergencies. This could be anything from a wedding gift to tires to the $250 deductible required by the emergency room when your son broke his leg playing baseball.

Expense	Amount
1.	
2.	
3.	
4.	
5.	

Now place a check mark next to the expenses you could have anticipated. Example: If one of the expenses you listed was tires for the car, you should have checked it. Tires wear out; that's a fact of life. Every time you drive your car, you are using up some of that tread. It's an expense you can anticipate because tires have a lifetime measured in miles.

Read or reread "Imagine This" on page 162 of the text. I think we can agree that this is never going to happen. Your mortgage company, or your landlord, is never going to switch you to one big annual payment. But just go with me on this. It's fun to think about how each of us would handle such a thing.

I have to admit that I'm a #1 kind of gal. That's my nature and a lot of the reason I got myself into so much trouble with money, credit, and debt (see chapter 1 if you do not recall). My first reaction would be one of giddy relief. In some insane way I would assume that I'd figure out how to pay that $12,000 later, but for now I have an extra $1,000 to use today.

Okay, now it's your turn. How did you respond? Explain.

She says:

He says:

While I'm sure you may have already figured this out, #3 is of course the correct answer. It does make a lot of sense. The good thing is that even if you are more prone to #1 or #2, just seeing how #3 works is empowering. Almost makes you hope your landlord will decide to go with the one annual payment, doesn't it? Well, almost!

Did you or your parents ever belong to a Christmas Club? What are your recollections of how it worked, and what was the big payoff right before Christmas?

I understand that there are still a few banks and credit unions that offer Christmas Club memberships. However, it's nearly a thing of the past. When I asked my bank manager why they discontinued them, he said now that people have their credit cards, there's no need to save up ahead of time.

Do you agree that the failure to anticipate can be very expensive? If so, give one example from your lives.

The Freedom Account is one of the elements of debt-proof living. It is a simple, personal management tool that makes unexpected, irregular, and intermittent expenses as ordinary, predictable, and necessary as your rent or grocery bill. It turns the unexpected into something you anticipate on a monthly basis. Your Freedom Account is going to put you in charge of funding your own emergencies. This is key to helping you break your dependence on credit cards.

What is the definition of *unexpected, irregular,* and *intermittent* expenses (p. 163)?

Remember: An expense that recurs every month *is not* a candidate for your Freedom Account.

How to start:

Step 1. _____

Even though you may be thinking that you cannot do this Freedom Account thing now because you just don't have enough money, put that thought out of your mind. I want you to develop your Freedom Account. It will not cost you a dime to do this "set up" work. We'll worry about funding it later. For now it is important that you do the work.

The goal in Step 1 is to determine the irregular, intermittent, and unexpected expenses you have had in the last year or so. This will give you a good idea of what you need to anticipate will happen in the future. While not a perfect predictor, the past is a good indicator because history does repeat itself. List the nature of the expense and then an estimate of how much that was on an annual basis. Example:

Expense	Annually	Monthly

There is no limit to the number of categories you can have in your Freedom Account; however, at this point I suggest you keep it to five or six of your most pressing irregular expenses. Refer to page 164 in the text for an idea of the basic types of expenses that belong in your Freedom Account. Notice how each has an annualized figure as well as a per month number. Arrive at this by simply dividing the annual amount by twelve.

Add together the monthly amounts to come up with one number. The example in the text on page 164 came to $345. This is the total of the monthly figures for the six Freedom Account subaccounts.

Step 2. _____

This is the point where many people deviate from the Freedom Account rules. This is one time in the debt-proof living process that you should not deviate at all. Trying to take shortcuts in this particular situation will only mess you up in the long run. Trust me on this, and open a second checking account. If your bank or credit union offers an interest-bearing checking account, that is the type of account you want to open. You will not earn interest until the balance reaches a certain level, but that's okay. If you can get an even better deal, but there are restrictions (like you can only write ten checks a month for example), go for that too. This will not be a seriously active account. You want to order checks for this new account. Be sure to have them personalized in both of your names, adding a special line that says, "Freedom Account."

Should you accept overdraft protection, ATM privileges, or a debit card for your new Freedom Account (page 165)? _____

Step 3. _____

This is important, so follow closely: At the time you open this account, request an automatic deposit authorization form. Fill it out. This is your directive to automatically transfer the amount you determine ($345 is the example from the text) from your regular account where you deposit your paychecks into your Freedom Account. Be careful when you select the date you want this transfer to occur. You might want to make it a day or two after payday to allow for holidays and weekends. The bank is not going to forget to do this, so you don't want to run the risk of bouncing checks on yourself.

Step 4. _____

Even in these days of high-tech computers and fancy software, sometimes keeping things really basic helps to keep them simple. I suggest you get a three-ring binder to care for your new Freedom Account. Make copies of the simple form at the end of this chapter—one page for each of your expenses or "subaccounts." Fill in the title of the subaccount plus the amount you will add to it each month (in the upper right corner). Punch holes in these sheets, and arrange them in order of urgency, putting the most urgent in the front.

Step 5. _____

Each month on the day your automatic transfer is made, deduct your Freedom Account transfer from your regular checking account just as if you paid a regular monthly bill. It will be the same every month. You will get used to it just as you got used to your rent and car payment.

Describe how you think you may feel to have a new monthly expense. Will you feel ripped off that you paid the money but didn't get anything in return, or will you feel righteous because you are doing the right thing by managing your money? Or is it something altogether different? Be brutally honest, and don't be surprised when your responses are, well . . . different. (Just like the two of you!)

He says:

She says:

Next go to your Freedom Account notebook and enter the individual deposits on each page and calculate the new balances.

Reread pages 166–68 in the text to see how Bob and Sally Brown managed and implemented their Freedom Account.

Reread the two sections on pages 169–171. Now list accounts you would like to add to your Freedom Account that will fulfill your dreams and your need for some money to call your own.

She says:

He says:

Pillow Talk

Identify several events in your future that you know will have a significant financial impact: Christmas, property taxes, college tuition, etc. Now imagine you have already accumulated the money. It's earmarked and in the bank just waiting for the due dates to arrive. Tell each other how you think that is going to feel and the impact it will have on your marriage. Now renew your commitment to do whatever it takes to make this happen.

Freedom Account

$ per month _____

Account Name

Date	Description	In	Out	Balance

17

You Can Get Out of Debt, Yes You Can!

If you held me in a hammerlock and forced me to name my favorite of the four debt-proof living elements, it would the Rapid Debt-Repayment Plan (RDRP). You'll be happy to know that the work required to develop your RDRP will not be as challenging as the work required to develop the spending records of the first element. And unlike elements two and three (the Contingency Fund and Freedom Account), the RDRP will not require you to come up with "new" funds before you can implement it.

Your RDRP will take the unsecured debts that you have right now along with what you are paying on them right now (even if that is only the bare minimum payments required by your creditors) and sprinkle fairy dust all over them. Okay, that's a little dramatic, and I can't honestly say the RDRP will make them magically disappear, but the rapidity with which full payment occurs is truly, in my opinion, magical.

The RDRP is a major element in the whole concept of debt-proof living for several reasons:

1. The RDRP gets rid of the heavy burden of high interest consumer debt that is weighing you down.
2. The RDRP frees up all that money you've been paying in interest and puts it back into your pockets. It's like giving yourselves a raise.
3. The RDRP gives you still another delicious taste of being in control of your finances and the joy of being good stewards of the money you have.

The RDRP is designed to take care of your unsecured debts. These are your debts that are not collateralized. The quick test to see if a debt is secured or unsecured is to ask this question: What is the consequence of nonpayment? If the answer includes the lender coming and repossessing something, then the debt is *secured*. The "something" is the collateral that guarantees the lender will be made whole even if you are unable to pay.

Mark "U" for unsecured and "S" for secured before each of the debts listed below:

_____ Home mortgage

_____ Credit cards

_____ Student loan

_____ Car loan

_____ Loan from Dad

_____ HEL (Home equity loan)

_____ HELOC (Home equity line of credit)

_____ Money owing the IRS

_____ Other: _____

For each one that you designated as a secured loan, go back and describe the collateral that is at risk if you were to default on that obligation.

Make a quick calculation of the total amount of money you are paying each month on your unsecured debts including principal and interest. Write the number here: $_____

Okay, let's have a little fun. Let's say that last month you finished paying off that last nickel of your unsecured debt. This month the monthly amount you filled in the blank several sentences above is now yours to manage. What will you do with it? Think carefully, dream joyfully, and then write your response below.

Beyond just the dollars and cents you will now have to devote to some other purpose, what other benefits can you imagine will come with your new "debt-free" status?

In the example on page 174, the Browns' total minimum payments in the month they commenced their RDRP was $430. Pull out all of your unsecured debts, and add up the minimum amount you are required to pay this month: $_____.

This is a very important number. You need to focus on it and memorize it because it is not going to change until you are completely free of your unsecured debts. That's because right now you are going to "fix" that total payment—it will not go down until you are done in the same way the Browns eventually "fixed" their payment at $430.

This will become a new monthly fixed payment on your Spending Plan, which is coming soon in chapter 18. Think of it the same way you think of your car payment or your rent. It's big, it's ugly, and it's yours for the foreseeable (and relatively short) future.

Reread the RDRP rules on pages 174–76. Now summarize each of the rules below:

Rule #1:

Rule #2:

Rule #3:

Rule #4:

Is it effective to follow only one or two of the rules?

What would have been the effect if the Browns followed only rules #1 and #2?

Now it's time to develop your own unique Rapid Debt-Repayment Plan.

Rule #1. No more new debt. This means you must immediately stop adding any new purchases to any of your unsecured debts. You cannot put out a raging fire if you continue to pour gasoline on it. You cannot stop your bathtub from overflowing unless you turn off the tap. You cannot get out of debt unless you stop adding to it. If you do not stop incurring new debt, this plan, or any other plan, will never work for you. You will go to your grave in perma-debt, which is a depressing thought but something you need to consider. Below write your collective commitment to no more new unsecured debt.

Rule #2. Fix your payments, and pay that same amount every month until all of your debts are paid. Make a list of the payments you must make (or have made) in this month on your credit cards, store charge cards, installment loans, and personal loans. Include medical and dental payments, student loans—every unsecured debt for which you are currently responsible to make payments. Add together all of these minimum payments, and circle the total. That is the amount you will pay every month.

Rule #3. Determine the number of payments required to pay each debt in full, and then arrange them in the order they will be paid off. Answer this question for each of your debts: How many months will it take us to reach $0 on each of our debts if we add no more new purchases and pay each month the same amount we will pay (or did pay) this month? This is tricky because of that annoying interest, but you can come up with that number for each of your debts. Either find a financial calculator (more on that in a moment) or get a lot of paper and set aside a few hours or more to figure it by hand as follows:

- Select one of your debts.
- Multiply its current balance by the annual percentage rate (APR) and divide the quotient by twelve. This will tell you how much of the next monthly payment will be allocated to interest.
- Now deduct that interest amount from the required payment. The result is the amount your principal balance will be reduced once you make that payment.

Now you have a new balance for next month.

- Repeat the process.
- Multiply by the APR, divide by twelve, subtract from the monthly payment, and subtract the result from the current balance to determine the new balance. And on and on until you reach $0.
- Now add up how many times you had to do that, and you'll have the number of months it will take to pay that debt in full.
- Do this for each of your debts.

Rule #4. As one debt is paid, take that payment and redirect it to the regular payment of the next debt in line. This is where the rapidity comes in because now you are prepaying your debts with payments far greater than required. But still your total monthly debt payment remains the same. This is the key to getting out of debt fast.

If you are balking at the idea of concentrating on the shortest debt first (not necessarily the one with the highest interest rate), understand that there's a good reason: You are going to need a big emotional payoff as soon as possible. Reaching that first $0 is going to give you an emotional payoff like you never dreamed possible. You need a plan that works and one that you will stick with. This is it. Believe me.

Developing your RDRP by hand is not impossible, but it is tedious. This is why we created the Rapid Dept-Repayment Plan Calculator which is a member benefit for *Cheapskate Monthly* online subscribers (www.cheapskate monthly.com). You simply input your current balances, interest rates, and current payment. One click produces your custom RDRP showing the exact month you will be debt-free. It also shows you how much you will save in the future if you begin saving your total payments once you are debt-free. It is truly remarkable and will inspire you to get into a RDRP frame of mind . . . now! Visit the website for a demonstration and more information.

Take a look at the RDRP example below, a different example than the one you see in the text. By following the rules, the entire debt is repaid in just eighteen months. This same debt load, paid back according to the creditor's plan, would have taken more than twenty-two years!

Rapid Dept-Repayment Plan

Debts are arranged in the order of the number of months required to pay them off with the shortest in the first position, not according to the interest rate or outstanding balance.

Wow! The first zero balance after only 3 months! Time for a small celebration.

MasterCard gets $145 this month which is the regular $120 payment plus the $25 that went to JCPenney previously.

Creditor	# Mos	$$ Bal	%	Payment Month																		
				4/03 #1	5/03 #2	6/03 #3	7/03 #4	8/03 #5	9/03 #6	10/03 #7	11/03 #8	12/03 #9	1/04 #10	2/04 #11	3/04 #12	4/04 #13	5/04 #14	6/04 #15	7/04 #16	8/04 #17	9/04 #18	10/04 #19
JCPenney	3	71		25	25	23	0															
MasterCard	8	1,000		120	120	122	145	145	145	145	124	0										
VISA	10	498		40	40	40	40	40	40	40	61	185	12	0								
Orthodontist	15	1,850		80	80	80	80	80	80	80	80	80	253	265	265	265	265	104	0			
Discover	18	1,497		55	55	55	55	55	55	55	55	55	55	55	55	55	55	216	320	320	79	0
Totals		4,916		320	320	320	320	320	320	320	320	320	320	320	320	320	320	320	320	320	79	0

The total of the minimum monthly payments in the first month is $320. This becomes a fixed monthly expense and should be entered on the Monthly Spending Plan.

In month #11 the orthodontist receives his regular $80 payment plus $185 which used to go to JCPenney, MasterCard, and VISA for a total of $265.

Debt-Free!

Rapid Dept-Repayment Plan Worksheet

Okay, now it's your turn. Use this worksheet to get started. . . .

In this column write the current minimum monthly payment for each of yor unsecured debts.

Creditor	# Mos	$$ Bal	%	Payment Month																		
				#1	#2	#3	#4	#5	#6	#7	#8	#9	#10	#11	#12	#13	#14	#15	#16	#17	#18	#19
Totals																						

Enter the total of your monthly payments here! This is your monthly debt payment. Enter it on your Monthly Spending Plan this month and every month until you're done.

There is nothing magical about 18 months—that's all this page allows. Your plan may take fewer or more months. But whatever the number of months, you will know exactly when you will be debt-free! Now it's time for you to develop your RDRP!

So, you have a few questions about the Rapid Debt-Repayment Plan? I thought you might . . .

You have been answering so many questions; you need a break. So you ask the questions, and I'll give the answers for a change.

The Rapid Debt-Repayment Plan always generates a lot of questions, not because it's so difficult to understand, but because it is so amazing. I love to see the look on the faces of people who see for the first time how it works. It's that moment of "getting it" that is so great.

It's not that the RDRP is such a difficult concept. Actually it's very simple. The RDRP reverses compounding interest (which by the way Einstein called the Eighth Wonder of the World) that creditors rely on to create huge income streams. It puts that concept to work *for* you instead of *against* you the way it has been working in the past.

Q: We want to do this, but we're not sure we can stop using our credit cards.

A: Well, *if that's the case,* you're only wasting your time by hanging around here. This is serious business. The RDRP is not for those who will not turn loose of the plastic. It takes a lot of courage to say "No more! We are not going to incur new debt." That's the attitude you must have to make this work.

If, on the other hand, you choose to change your attitude to "We are going to do this . . . we are determined, committed, 100 percent on board even though we're scared and a little shaky" . . . you're perfect candidates, and I cannot wait to watch your progress!

Q: We think the debt with the highest interest rate should be in the #1 spot. That's what we've always heard is the right way to do it. Besides it's the one costing us the most so that only makes sense.

A: There are some "experts" who insist you must pay off your highest interest debt first, but quite frankly I don't put much stock in that advice. It's a good theory because on paper it makes sense. But they are only looking at the numbers. There's more to devising a brilliant plan than just figuring out the mathematics. You need a plan you can be confident will actually work.

You are going to need incremental rewards in the form of emotional boosts . . . and you need to start getting them as quickly as possible. You need that great feeling of paying a debt in full (we call that achieving a "zero balance") and you need it soon . . . if not sooner!

Let me pose this scenario: Your highest interest rate debt is also your largest debt. It's huge . . . like $16,500 at 18 percent interest. You could go *years* without hitting that first zero. How long do you think you'd stick with that plan? Let me guess: not long. You'd give up and chuck the entire highest-interest-rate-first plan those "experts" recommend because it is missing that emotional reward aspect.

This expert (yes, that would be me) is telling you that the RDRP works. And quite frankly, in your position at this time, I think you deserve a workable plan, not just one that looks good on paper. Thousands of people have proven it works, and I believe you are going to prove it too. That's how much faith I have in you.

I've played with the RDRP Calculator till I was just sure I'd worn it out (not possible, but that's how it felt). Let me assure you that the difference between putting your highest interest debt in the #1 spot or doing it my way—which of course is the *right* way—is miniscule in the end. Most of the time, the difference is a month or two in the payoff period, if that. But the real difference? The RDRP is a doable plan because it has both a financial and emotional payoff. It's a plan you can finish . . . and that, my friends, is the invaluable aspect of the RDRP. And more than that, it looks good posted on the fridge.

Now that I've made that big explanation, I'll tell you that I have great respect for experts who insist you work on your highest interest debts first. I don't agree with them, but I respect their position. That's why we have added an option to the RDRP Calculator that allows you to override the calculator's order. (Still, I suggest you not do that!)

Q: We just can't start our RDRP right now because we don't have any extra money. We can barely pay our bills as it is.

A: You make a statement that many people make, and quite frankly I don't understand. Really! I don't understand what you're talking about. Either you have not read chapter 17 carefully or you read it with a closed mind. You assume that you must have additional money over and above what you are paying on your bills right now, this very month. Your assumption is wrong!

Read this again: The RDRP does not require that you come up with any additional money over the minimum payments you were required to pay this month. Now repeat after me: "The RDRP is based on our current minimum monthly payments—the amounts we paid to each of our creditors this month."

With your RDRP, if the minimum payment on your Visa account was $24 this month, it's going to be $24 next month. I know you can pay that because it's the amount you paid this month. See? The RDRP does not require that you add anything to the minimum payment that was required this month. However, if you could not even pay the minimum required this month, then you have a different problem.

Bottom line: You have *no excuse* for not starting right now, this month. Even if you continue to say you cannot do it yet, I have news for you. You're already doing it! If you are making your minimum payments, you have in effect checked off the first month on the RDRP chart. You've already begun . . . you are on your way!

Q: We have one account that has two (or three?) different interest rates. There's one rate for Cash Advances, another for Balance Transfers, and another for New Purchases. We have balances under all three headings, so which interest rate should we enter into the RDRP calculator?

A: If you're brave, use the highest interest rate for the entire balance, and you'll shorten the number of months required to pay that balance. The RDRP Calculator may require that you increase the payment some to adjust for the higher interest rate, but that's okay if you can swing it. Or average the rates to come up with a single rate. But be careful, if a large portion of your balance is subject to the highest rate, you might be underestimating. If you want to be as accurate as possible, you have to work out a "weighted" interest rate. For example, let's say you have a $2,500 balance on one of your accounts—$500 from a cash advance at 20 percent interest and $2,000 in purchases at 12 percent interest. That means that one-fifth of your balance is at 20 percent interest and four-fifths is at 12 percent.

Now you could warm up your algebra skills . . . or do what I do (actually a form of counting on my fingers): 20 + 12 + 12 + 12 + 12 = 68 divided by 5 = 13.6. That means my weighted average interest rate is 13.6 percent. That is the rate I will enter into the RDRP Calculator for that debt.

Q: What happens if the interest rates on one or more of our credit card accounts changes midstream?

A: Well, first I hope if your rates change, they are decreasing! (If you get an increase, fight it . . . , and please tell me it didn't happen because you were late with a payment . . . aaaughh!)

But back to your question: Any significant change along the way means you should toss your old plan and make a new RDRP. It's so simple with the RDRP Calculator you could do it every day. Just use your current balances (find them on your most current statements) as of the time you draw your new plan; use the new interest rate, *but keep the same base fixed monthly payments as you had on the original plan.*

Example: If in month one you paid $50 on your MasterCard and now the principal balance is way down, and the statement says all you have to pay next month is $28 . . . *ignore* that. Stick with the $50 you've been paying all along. Recap: Use the most current principal balance, the most current interest rate, but keep the original (old) monthly payment.

Q: Why can't we include our secured debts like a home equity loan, car loan, even our first mortgage in our RDRP? We want to see when we will be 100 percent free of all our debts!

A: I hear you, and I fully understand! However, you should not combine your debts into one plan because the RDRP Calculator cannot tell the difference between a secured and unsecured debt. If you dumped all of them into the same plan, it's possible it would put your home equity loan (a fifteen-year debt) ahead of say a Visa account. That wouldn't make sense to pay off your home equity loan first and push the high interest rate Visa to the end. If you don't understand that, don't worry. Just do as I suggest, and do not mix your secured debts with the unsecured.

Here's what you can do: Create a second Rapid Debt-Repayment Plan for your secured debts. Of course, you would work the plans simultaneously, but you would see exactly when that car will be paid, the home equity loan . . . even your mortgage. That's what I would suggest. It is empowering to begin with the end in mind.

Q: What's the difference between "fixed" and "falling" payments?

A: If your debt is structured so that the monthly payment is the same every month (like your mortgage or your car loan), that is a "fixed" payment. It doesn't matter how much you pay in a month or how much you prepay the principal, the monthly payment remains the same.

A "falling" payment would be like a credit card payment. You never know from one month what the required payment will be because it is calculated according to the current balance owing. Credit card accounts are a good example of "falling" payment loans.

Typically secured loans have fixed payments, unsecured have falling payments. But that's not in stone. It's possible that you have an unsecured loan from Uncle Guido. And he demands $100 a month until paid. Period. No questions, no excuses. That's a fixed payment unsecured loan.

You may have a home equity line of credit, and the payment each month is calculated on the current outstanding balance, which fluctuates as you withdraw funds. That's a secured debt with a "falling" payment structure.

In the first screen of the RDRP Calculator, where you input your data, you will be asked to specify if the payment is "fixed" or "falling." Mark them accordingly.

Note: The secret of the RDRP is that we choose to "fix" all "falling" payments. But the RDRP Calculator will do that for you. You don't have to worry.

Q: When we try to use the RDRP Calculator we keep getting a message that says "With the terms you've submitted you will never pay off this debt. You must increase the payment" or something like that. Why? We put in the minimum payment required by our creditor.

A: You got this message because the RDRP Calculator determined that the payment you inserted is less than even the interest required according to the terms you gave. That is not unusual! Creditors often (I could name names) love accepting interest only, or even less (converting unpaid interest into principal) because that guarantees you will never pay it off. The calculator does not lie. If you get that message, thank God! You've learned that you're digging a deeper hole than you realized. So go back and increase that payment by $5, and try again and again until you stop getting that message.

Q: I get an error message that contains "NaN . . ." when using the RDRP Calculator. What's up with that?

A: You've included something like a $ sign or a comma or a space in the calculator data. You cannot do that. Use only decimals as needed. Clean it up and try again.

Q: Okay, so I don't have to pay more than my current minimum monthly payments. But what if I want to? What if I want to speed things up and add say $50 a month to my plan? How would I do that?

A: We call this a monthly "booster." The Calculator gives you the opportunity to do this, although it is not required. When you get to the RDRP Calculator, you will see where to input this "booster" amount. Then the plan will distribute that $50 in the most effective way possible. If, in the future, you encounter tough times and you want to pull back and stop boosting with that $50 each month, just refigure your RDRP as explained above, leaving the $50 off. See? You are in charge here; you are managing your money, and boy, doesn't that feel great?

   If you are figuring your RDRP by hand, simply increase the payment of the debt that's in the #1 position by $50. Of course, that debt is going to reach $0 balance even more quickly, and then just keep moving the payment, including the $50, down to the next debt and the next and on and on.

   In the event you have a one-time booster, you'll have to refigure your plan twice, once before you make the booster and then again after to remove the booster.

Q: So what do I do when my RDRP is complete? Then what?

A: Well, first you have a celebration. Then you write me, so I can cheer too. Next you assess your wonderful options. Remember, debt steals options; paying off debt returns those options to you.

One of those options is to begin immediately saving/investing all of the money you've been pouring into your RDRP every month. The RDRP Calculator has a little surprise for you. At the end you will see a place to input that total of the payments you've been making, the current rate of interest you can expect, your current age, and the age at which you want to retire. Hit "compute," and you'll immediately find out how much money you can accumulate by simply saving that money every month. And why not? You've gotten out of the habit of spending that money, so moving it to a savings account or investment will be quite painless.

Wow, just wait until you see that total!

Pillow Talk

Compare how you feel right now about your debt situation compared to say a month ago before you began the project. Are you beginning to see a light at the end of a very dark tunnel? Let your spouse know how grateful you are that you are part of this team and not making the journey solo.

18

It's Not a Budget, Honestly!

Finally, you have made it to the much-anticipated chapter (please tell me you *have* been looking forward to this!) where we will assemble all the separate elements you've been building that remain disconnected like the pieces of a big puzzle.

Describe briefly the four elements of debt-proof living:

Monthly Spending Record:

Contingency Fund:

Freedom Account:

Rapid Debt-Repayment Plan:

Refer to Bob and Sally Brown's Monthly Spending Record (p. 182). It revealed that they severely overspent their income. How much were they over? _____

But to make matters even worse, they did not give any of their income to church or charity, they did not save, and they did not allocate any money for unexpected or irregular expenses they know will be coming in the future. You couldn't even say that they stayed afloat.

The problem is the $481.20 they overspent. Surely they could only do that by using credit to fill in the "gap" between what they spent and the money they had. By adding this much to their already substantial debt, what is a fair estimate of how much that $481.20 will become before they finally pay it back someday? $_____

So while we need to hand it to the Browns for tracking their spending, they have a lot of work to do.

Describe some of the steps the Browns took to get from what happened last month to what they plan to spend in the coming month (pp. 183–85).

The first step to drawing their first Monthly Spending Plan (p. 184) is to start by plugging in their fixed monthly expenses. This is where they begin to put the puzzle together.

First is a fixed expense of Giving. Next is their Contingency Fund fixed expense, their Freedom Account contribution (fixed because it will be the same every month), and their RDRP payment (again a fixed payment). Under that they account for their mortgage and car payment, which are both fixed expenses.

From there the Browns need to really tighten their belts. Looking at the Spending Record, they determine that some areas of their spending were completely out of control. What did they discover about fast food, and what do they plan to do the following month?

Do you think they did the right thing to *not* eliminate fast food altogether but to reduce it considerably to $75 for the month? Why or why not?

The chart on page 184 of the text shows the way the Browns plan to spend their money. This is how they started out the month. Separate from this chart, they continued to track their daily spending, creating their Weekly and Monthly Spending Record from which they will then discover how they did in actuality compared to what they intended. And all the while they're keeping on eye on their spending to see how it is lining up with what they've planned. The Monthly Spending Plan is broken out by week, so that makes it easier to watch how things are going.

The chart on page 187 shows their actual spending at the end of the month in each category. Those Browns are pretty disciplined, aren't they! I don't know if they were scared all month long to overspend or what, but the result is that they came in under their plan.

Now they are ready to go for the next month because they know what they spent and can reassess to make their Spending Plan for next month. And on it goes.

Keeping a Monthly Spending Plan is a lot of work. As it should be! Becoming a faithful and responsible money manager is not child's play. But it's not difficult work either. And it gets more enjoyable the more successful you are.

Have you had a division of labor discussion yet? Which of you, or both, will be handling the following financial tasks for now? Answer "He," "She," or "Both," keeping in mind that there is no correct answer. You should divide the tasks according to your abilities, talents, and strengths:

- Balancing the checkbooks each month (remember that now you have at least two): _____

- Managing the Freedom Account (includes posting deposits and checks written and keeping track of the Freedom Account checkbook): _____
_____

- Making the deposits into the Contingency Fund and keeping track of the monthly statements: _____

- Managing the RDRP: _____

- Managing the weekly and monthly Spending Records: _____

- Prepare your Balance Sheet and Statement of Net Worth once a year: _____

- Other, which is _____: _____
_____

You may wish to add other related tasks like gathering all the documentation to file your taxes or manage your 401(k) or other retirement plans.

Explain the Envelope Method. What are some of the circumstances that indicate this might be the best method for a couple? Do you see the Envelope Method as being right for you at this time?

Write a description of The Edge. Have you ever resided there? If so, what was (is) that like?

How can you build a wall of protection between yourselves and that scary place on the edge of financial devastation?

Describe the four Savings Levels and include how you will know it's time to move to the next level:

Savings Level 1:

Savings Level 2:

Savings Level 3:

Savings Level 4:

Pillow Talk

If you are feeling overwhelmed, discouraged, even sure you cannot do this because it's just too hard, have the courage to tell your spouse. Share your heart. And take the bold step of reconfirming your commitment to "Live the Plan" as a couple, no matter what, no matter how discouraged you get or how many times you fall flat on your faces. You will make it if you are diligent and promise to never give up.

Part 3

Unique Solutions for Common Dilemmas

19

Finding Money You Didn't Know You Had

Our fictitious couple, Bob and Sally Brown, in an effort to right the wrongs of their overspending, took a drastic step. They completely eliminated family and couple entertainment from their Spending Plan. Either they overlooked it completely or decided it was frivolous given their overspending of the previous month.

Do you believe that was the right thing to do? They did overspend by nearly $500, don't forget. If not, why not?

There are many ways to participate in entertaining activities without spending a lot of money. Most cities, especially during the summer months and in December, offer community events that are free or nearly so. What ideas would you offer the Browns for ways they could keep entertainment and fun in their lives without giving up their commitment to debt-proof their marriage?

Think about a time that you might have tried to fit into jeans or shoes that you could get on but were in truth just too small. How did that feel? How long did you tough it out before getting rid of them?

Remember that experience if you should try to cram yourselves into an unreasonably tight Spending Plan.

What is the way to make your Spending Plan more roomy (p. 196)?

Sure you read it and theoretically it sounds good, but at this point in your journey to debt-proof your marriage do you really believe that every-little-bit-counts when it comes to spending as well as saving?

If you are in unsecured debt, did that happen overnight? If not, explain.

There are some who believe they have only two choices: living deeply in debt or living like a pauper. Do you agree, or do you have a description for some place between? Explain.

Sometimes as we go through challenging times, it's helpful to spend time with others in the same situation. Do you think you could draw help, hope, and inspiration from other fellow "travelers" who are also debt-proofing their lives and their marriages? Or would it be too intimidating to share that part of your lives with anyone outside family?

"If you learn to keep a lid on your expenses by controlling your spending, something amazing will happen. You will reduce your needs. As you reduce your needs, you cut expenses, and that means you have more of your income to invest in your future" (p. 198). List ten ways you are fairly confident you can reduce your spending right away. For starters think of things you can do for yourselves that you are now paying others to do.

1.

2.

3.

4.

5.

6.

7.

8.

9.

10.

I would like to invite you to join other couples and individuals who are living the plan at *Cheapskate Monthly*. Don't worry about that word "cheapskate." It's an endearing term that means we give regularly, save consistently, and don't spend beyond our means. To do that, we are always looking for ways to reduce our expenses and improve our lives.

My subscription newsletter, *Cheapskate Monthly,* premiered in 1992. Filled with motivation, inspiration, and every idea you can imagine for how to live better and spend less, *Cheapskate Monthly* has been in continuous publication since the first issue. As our family of subscribers has increased, the newsletter has expanded too, and now we offer the newsletter online in electronic format as well as a very active website, *(www.cheapskatemonthly.com)*, which is filled with thousands of articles (many in the public area), searchable back issues, and more than three dozen calculators including the RDRP Calculator. I look forward to welcoming you to our cheapskate family!

Pillow Talk

You read about forty different ideas for plugging the money leaks in your household and lives. How many might be applicable to your lives? Talk about other places you can recover money that is leaking out of your household. Remember, nothing is too small or insignificant.

20

Credit: The Good, the Bad, the Ugly

Credit is not bad. It's the abuse of credit that results in debilitating unsecured debt that is the problem. That abuse ranges from its easy availability to outrageously high rates of interest and outlandish punitive fees. Credit, when used appropriately, can enhance your life. Abused, it can ruin it.

Larry Burkett, personal finance expert, says there are three basic principles for how credit should be used.[1]

1. Credit should be rare—your last option not the first.
2. Credit should be taken for the shortest possible term and repaid quickly.
3. Never take on debt without an absolutely certain way to pay. Only secured credit provides this kind of certainty.

In what ways does revolving credit card debt violate Burkett's principles?

Credit is like a rope. As a tool it can be very useful in your life, or you can tie it into a noose to hang yourself. Give one example of the way credit can be a useful tool and one way it can be more like a hanging noose.

Why do you need one, good, all-purpose credit card?

What are the characteristics of a good, all-purpose credit card?

Define "twenty-five-day grace period."

On page 214 of the text, "How to use it," are basic guidelines for the safe and sane way to manage a credit card account. Using these, what are the guidelines the two of you have agreed upon for the care of your one, good, all-purpose credit card?

What is an effective way you can be covered in the event of an authentic emergency without carrying that credit card in your wallet or purse (p. 215)?

Why is it dangerous to carry a credit card, particularly when you are still carrying revolving credit card debt?

You need to pull out all of your credit cards and divide them into two piles. By what criteria should you separate them?

What is the procedure to follow for those with $0 balances?

How about the ones with balances?

What are the potential hazards of closing a credit card account while a balance remains (p. 217)?

Why is it dangerous to play the "balance transfer" game (pp. 217–18)?

What are the three common reasons so many of us prefer just about anything other than seeing what's on our credit reports? Name them and explain:

1.

2.

3.

What is a credit bureau?

What are the five types of information included on a credit report?

1.

2.

3.

4.

5.

How can you get a copy of your credit report?

Why are multiple inquiries considered a negative on a credit report (p. 222)?

Other than being denied for new credit, what results can a person expect for having bad credit (p. 223)?

Why do you need to take an aggressive position as manager of your own credit reports?

What is generally considered an okay credit score (p. 224)?

How often can you expect your credit score to change?

What are several of the more common reasons for a low score?

What is the process called that allows you to challenge the information on your credit report?

How would you go about disputing an entry on your credit report?

What does the law require a credit-reporting agency to do once it receives your request for reinvestigation (p. 228)?

Pillow Talk

How do you feel about having just one good, all-purpose credit card between the two of you? Share your fears, joys, concerns . . . whatever they are and come up with a plan or a compromise that makes both of you feel comfortable. Then stick with it.

21

Tell the Middleman, Thanks but No Thanks!

In the same way you can experience dramatic results by rapidly repaying your unsecured debts, you can save a lot of money by rapidly prepaying your mortgage. It's such a remarkably effective way to avoid paying a lot of interest that third parties, sometimes called middlemen, like to get involved. These third party companies offer to set you up on a biweekly program, collect your payments, and pay the lender on your behalf.

Many lenders, taking their cues from the "middlemen," have created their own accelerated programs by offering biweekly plans directly to their customers.

What is the secret that makes the "biweekly mortgage payment" work to the borrower's advantage (p. 232)?

What is the overall effect of paying the equivalent of an extra mortgage payment (thirteen rather than twelve) every year (p. 233)?

Why do mortgage lenders and other companies offer biweekly programs to people like you and the Wheelers?

1. Because they truly care about homeowners and want to demonstrate compassion by helping them repay their loans years earlier.
2. Because they've had a change of heart about charging so much interest, and this is their way of giving their borrowers a rebate.
3. Because these biweekly programs add to lenders' profit margins.

Are biweekly programs like the Equity Accelerator the Wheelers were offered scams?

What are the advantages of doing the equivalent of a biweekly program yourselves directly with your lender and without a middleman?

How can the Wheelers do this themselves?

Other than keeping them in control of their own accelerated payment schedule, what advantages will the Wheelers realize when they set up their own program?

What is the difference between "paying down" and "paying ahead" (p. 235)?

You want to reduce the principal balance on your mortgage. What instruction should you give the lender?

You want to send in several mortgage payments so you can go on vacation without having to remember to make your payments while you're gone. What instruction should you give the lender?

Why is it important that you give clear instructions whenever you make unscheduled or irregular payments on a loan?

Pillow Talk

On a scale of 1 to 10 where 1 means "It's not even on the radar screen," and 10 is "We're already doing this!" where does the suggestion of prepaying your mortgage come on your plan to debt-proof your marriage? Discuss.

22

How to Stay on Track
with a Roller-Coaster Income

If you have ever depended on self-employment income, it's likely you know both financial thrill and agony. It is likely you assumed because of your unpredictable income, you could not really live according to a Spending Plan. Good news: You are wrong. You can learn how to stay on track even when your self-employment income derails from time to time.

Our definition of self-employed is a person whose income is pretty much a mystery from month to month. Self-employeds do not know for sure when or how much they'll get paid. Surprisingly, it's not only those who own their own businesses who are technically self-employed. List the different titles of the self-employed.

Are you currently self-employed according to this definition?

Many self-employed people have flawed thinking. They assume that they can multiply their best month by _____ to predict their annual income.

Why should every self-employed household have a separate checking account for his or her self-employment income even if one spouse is self-employed and the other receives a regular salary?

In what ways must self-employeds exercise even greater self-control than a person with a predictable paycheck?

The key to surviving the self-employed roller coaster is to determine the monthly salary the Employer can afford to pay the Employee. Should this be the most the Employer can afford or the least the Employee can survive on? Explain your answer.

TO DO

Create a simple ledger and record the "deposits" and "paychecks" for the scenario outlined on page 241 to get a visual illustration for how to survive the Self-Employment Roller Coaster.

How would you advise the couple whose self-employed income month after month is not sufficient to cover their bare-bones, just-the-essentials, absolutely minimum needs?

1. You have too much invested to give up, so borrow wherever and whatever you can to hang on. Things are bound to turn around soon.

2. Close it down and file bankruptcy to "stop the bleeding" and to protect the few assets you may have remaining.
3. Get a real job and shift your self-employed endeavor to side-job status because even if it cannot support you it offers you great tax benefits.

Marc Eisenson, coauthor of *Invest in Yourself*, would answer "3" without hesitation. "Our favorite game plan for hedging your bets is having an 'Ace in the Hole,' a very small business (or two) that you start on the cheap. For some, it becomes the stepping-stone to a new career, for others it's a sideline that offers both extra income and welcome tax deductions. Everyone we know who's got an Ace feels more secure for having it."[1]

What are three pieces of advice a self-employed couple or individual should take to help smooth out the extremes of the self-employed roller-coaster ride (p. 242)?

1.

2.

3.

Pillow Talk

Discuss the pros and cons of being self-employed. If you are not now, have either of you ever had such aspirations? Talk about your tolerance for the thrill and the agony of a roller-coaster ride.

What to Do When You've Fallen and You Can't Get Up

Over the years I have corresponded with many couples who have dug themselves out of the pit of financial despair through a process known as credit counseling. Over those same years, the credit counseling industry has changed drastically.

Briefly describe what credit counseling is and who it is for.

In a credit counseling situation, there are three parties. Name them:

1.

2.

3.

The way to measure if counseling is successful is to check to see who benefits from it. In a successful transaction, how do the three parties benefit?

1. The consumer?

2. The creditor?

3. The credit counselor?

List several of the ways that a nonprofit corporation can operate just like a for-profit (p. 244).

Describe the main difference between a for-profit corporation and one that is organized and incorporated not-for-profit (p. 244).

Does this surprise you?

What exactly is credit counseling (p. 244)?

Typically which types of debts will a credit counseling organization assist with?

Are the better credit counselors successful with reducing the principal owed by their clients?

If a client is accepted into a debt-management program, what should they expect and how does it work?

Most credit counseling organizations receive revenue from two sources within the counseling process. What are they?

Do you see any problem with that?

Does credit counseling have any potential long-term side effects?

On page 246, credit counseling is likened to what serious medical treatment?

For a couple to be likely candidates for credit counseling, what symptoms or effects of debt should they be experiencing (p. 247)?

Do credit counseling organizations have the choice to report to or withhold information from the credit bureaus about their clients?

How do the credit bureaus find out if a person is in counseling, and does this information have negative connotations on that person's credit history?

What is one of the ways the credit counseling industry will be impacted if and when the pending Bankruptcy Reform Act of 2003 is signed into law?

Briefly describe "debt negotiation."

Is debt negotiation a regulated profession requiring that certified negotiators comply with federal statutes?

What are some of the problems associated with debt negotiation that sounds oh, so easy in the commercials?

Briefly review five things debt negotiators probably won't tell you:

1.

2.

3.

4.

5.

Are there ever times that debt negotiation might be appropriate and beneficial to both parties? If yes, what are they?

Credit counseling should be seen as a last resort to avoid filing for bankruptcy. Are there any reasonable alternatives to consider if things have not become that bad (p. 252)? If so, what are they?

Pillow Talk

Are there any conditions you can think of that would prompt you to contact a creditor and offer to settle for less than the full amount you now owe? Don't take this too seriously. It's prudent to consider "what if" situations occasionally.

24

A Call to Faithfulness

I'm banking on the expectation that you won't skip over this chapter. As anxious as you may be to start finding all the money that's leaking out of your lives and to get your Contingency Fund and Freedom Account activated, I think it is important that you consider some of the deeper issues of your lives.

What is your definition of "wealth"?

Are you wealthy now? What is the evidence of that?

If not, how will you recognize it when you are?

"True wealth is a holistic sense of overall well-being that no amount of money alone can buy. Money is just a tool that we can use to become wealthy. This sense of well-being gets to the deeper issues of our lives—our personal values" (p. 254). Do you agree with that statement? Explain.

The Bible, the best-selling book of all time (Did you know that? It's true), has more passages about what topic than any other? _____

What is the second most dominant theme? _____
(Clearly I was not the first to write a book on love and money!)
Referring to pages 254–56 of the text (there are plenty more references where those came from . . . , so feel free to add a few of your own), what does the Bible say about the following:

Charity:

Repaying debt:

Relationship between creditor and debtor:

Savings:

Investing:

Diversifying your investments:

Managing your financial risk:

Financial planning:

Giving (tithing):

Stewardship:

How do you respond to the universal law that everything you own is on loan from God?

Why should God trust you with any more money than he's given you to manage in the past?

I hate to get personal, but using the current condition of your car as an indicator for how you take care of your personal finances, what's the verdict?

Do you agree with my old boss's general rule of thumb that the way you care for your possessions is an indicator for how you will care for what belongs to others?

In his book *The Purpose Driven Life*, Rick Warren says, "Most people fail to realize that money is both a test and a trust from God. God uses finances to teach us to trust him and for many people, money is the greatest test of all. God watches how we use money to test how trustworthy we are."[1]

Think back over the past month. What kind of a grade would you give yourselves in God's course Faithful Steward 101?

God is long-suffering and patient. He allows us to make our stupid mistakes, to not trust him, to think we know best, to run ahead of him, and to try to take care of our lives and our emergencies by ourselves. We try to level all the bumps in the road. And when we stumble and fall despite our foolish efforts, he doesn't give up on us. Never! He forgives and gives us another chance. And another, and another.

You can count on God to keep his promises. Now the question is can he count on you to be faithful?

Write a summary paragraph that expresses your response and commitment.

Pillow Talk

Faithfulness. What does it mean to you both in your relationship with your spouse and your relationship with God, both individually and as a couple? If you've never thought about this specifically in the past, take the leap of faith and talk about it now.

25

Couples like You

Who doesn't love a good story? But what makes a good story great for me is when I can personally identify with the people and circumstances and believe by the time I finish reading that if they can do this or that, then so can I.

Probably the best payoff for what I've been privileged to do over the past decade is the mail I receive. Much of it comes in the form of progress reports and "Turning Point" stories—readers' personal accounts of struggle, success, and hope. I love to know how people just like you are overcoming life's challenges, debt-proofing their lives, and putting their marriages and families back together.

In chapter 25 Tim and Belinda, Renee and Joseph, Nancy and Richard, and Kevin and Sondra tell their stories. Did you identify with any (or all) of these couples? If so, explain.

In their story Renee says there's a huge, generally accepted misconception that if you are a physician you are automatically wealthy and have no financial problems. Is that something you've pretty much assumed as well? Will you in the future? Describe your thoughts and feelings.

Did any of the stories encourage you to believe "If they can do it, so can we"? If so, which one, and what specifically about that couple spoke to you in that way?

In preparing for this project, I asked members of my *Cheapskate Monthly* family to participate in a focus group. I want to give you an opportunity to participate in a similar way. The questionnaire that follows is the same one the focus group couples received and responded to. I hope the questions will help to stimulate your thinking in ways perhaps you have not considered before and that will help you as you set out to debt-proof your marriage. And I hope that one day you will write your story.

Pillow Talk

Some of us are more private than others. When you are debt-free, will one or both of you be anxious to write your story for others to read, or will you want to keep this completely private? Talk about that, listing reasons pro and con.

Questionnaire

1. How long did you know each other before you married?

2. Did you talk about money before you married? For example: Who would manage it and how that would be done? Did you establish any principles, values, ideals? If yes, what were they generally?

3. Did you personally bring any money "baggage" to the marriage (debt, money secrets, ruined credit)?

4. What money fantasies or money myths did you bring to your marriage?

5. What was your perception of the money management style of the home in which you grew up? Who handled the family's money; who paid the bills; who earned the living; were you privy to fights about money; did this information cause you to worry?

6. Did you assume your money role in your marriage would be the same as the home in which you grew up? Example: "My mother didn't have to worry about money, so I just assumed that my husband would take care of everything in the same way that my father did."

7. "In every marriage there is a saver and a spender." Does your marriage fit that statement? If so, which are you? Explain.

8. Describe your perception of your spouse's money style or personality.

9. What about your partner's money style used to (may still) drive you nuts? Does she or he know that?

10. Have conflicts over money affected other areas of your lives and relationships?

11. What was your perception of consumer credit when you married? Was it a good thing, get all you can, it's an entitlement, if they'll give it to us it must be okay, etc.?

12. Describe the money conflicts in your marriage and your reaction to them (blame, resentment, anger, fear). Do you have any specific instances or situations you can tell about? How did that make you feel?

13. Describe one or two of your worst money blunders as a couple. As an individual.

14. How bad (if at all) did your financial situation get?

15. Statistics indicate that 90 percent of all divorces find their roots in unresolved conflicts over money. Would you agree with that statement? How close did you come to being part of that statistic?

16. What was your turning point? Describe the event(s). How bad did it have to get for you to be willing to participate in some kind of change?

17. Was there a spiritual dimension to your financial turnaround? If yes, please describe.

18. How do you manage your finances today? Who handles the day-by-day management of your money, Contingency Fund, Freedom Account, checkbooks, etc.?

19. Have you established any limits, boundaries, or specific guidelines for the management of your money? What are they?

20. Describe your life now—occupations, family, goals, and dreams.

21. If an engaged couple asked you to counsel them regarding money and marriage, what would you tell them?

Conclusion

You have come to the end of this workbook, but it could be the beginning of a new stage in your marriage. At the very least you'll never again look at the money in your marriage in the same way. More than anything, I hope that, as you read, something spoke to your hearts and will continue to resonate in your minds.

I've done my part. Now it's up to you to take what you've learned and release it into your marriage and your lives.

I refuse to say good-bye. Instead I'm inviting you to visit me soon and often at www.cheapskatemonthly.com. We have created a special "wing" of the site devoted solely to couples just like you who are in every imaginable stage and phase of debt-proofing their marriages.

I've left space below for both of you to write a statement of intent (you could call this the P.S. for your wedding vows). Start with, "I am ready to . . ." Of course, this will be private between only the two of you. But in my heart, I'm hoping you'll end it with, ". . . until death do us part."

Notes

Chapter 20   Credit: The Good, the Bad, the Ugly

1. Larry Burkett, *The Word on Finances* (Chicago: Moody, 1994), 146.

Chapter 22   How to Stay on Track with a Roller-Coaster Income

1. Marc Eisenson, et al., *Invest in Yourself* (New York: John Wiley & Sons, 1998), 143.

Chapter 24   A Call to Faithfulness

1. Rick Warren, *The Purpose Driven Life: What on Earth Am I Here For?* (Grand Rapids: Zondervan, 2002), 36.